Beyond Code

Beyond Code

Context, Constraints, and the New Craft of Software

Jeremy McEntire

CAGE & MIRROR PUBLISHING

ISBN: 979-8-9949685-2-9

First Edition

Cover design by Jeremy McEntire

Printed in the United States of America

Contents

Preface

The tutorials on how to use a specific AI coding tool will expire with the next model release. The predictions about what AI will do next will expire faster than that. This book teaches neither. It teaches the physics of software engineering: the forces that govern coordination, verification, and specification regardless of which tools exist and which predictions prove correct. Those forces do not expire.

Software engineering has always been a coordination problem disguised as a coding problem, and the disguise held for sixty years because code was expensive enough to dominate every conversation about productivity. AI stripped the disguise away. The cost of producing code collapsed by an order of magnitude, and what remained, visible for the first time, was the essential complexity that was always there: understanding what to build, determining whether it is correct, and managing what happens when systems grow beyond what any single person can hold in mind. The industry is now discovering, with some discomfort, that these problems are harder than the coding ever was, and that no tool eliminates them, because they are not inefficiencies to be optimized away. They are the physics of the discipline.

The book is organized in six parts. The first establishes what changed when code production became cheap and what happens when teams attempt to use AI without understanding the forces that govern their work. The second and third examine context and constraints: how to construct the information environment that determines output quality, and how to specify boundaries that make output correct by construction rather than by luck. The fourth addresses coordination across agents, human and artificial. The fifth turns to the human craft: the cognitive and organizational skills that determine whether an engineer can operate effectively in this landscape. The sixth examines what is changing, what is not, and what engineers become when the underlying physics is understood.

The argument is cumulative. Each chapter builds on the preceding chapters, and the later chapters assume familiarity with the concepts and evidence established earlier. The evidence comes from controlled experiments in multi-agent AI coordination, from published research in information theory, cognitive science, and organizational behavior, and from engineering coaching transcripts that illustrate how the theoretical principles manifest in the daily practice of working engineers. The transcripts have been anonymized: names, companies, and identifying details have been changed, and the individuals involved have given permission for their use.

Two absences are worth noting. The book does not contain step-by-step instructions for using any specific AI tool, because the tools change faster than books can be printed and instructions that expire are worse than no instructions at all. The book does not contain reassurance that your current skills and your current role will survive the transition intact, because the honest assessment of the trajectory does not support that reassurance and this book does not offer comfort it cannot justify. What it contains is the physics that governs the landscape regardless of which tools exist and which roles survive, and the argument that understanding that physics is the most durable foundation available for whatever comes next.

PART I

The Shift

CHAPTER 1

The Inversion

In mid-2025, a research organization called METR conducted one of the only controlled experiments on whether AI coding tools make experienced software developers faster. They recruited sixteen seasoned open-source contributors, people who averaged five years and fifteen hundred commits on their respective projects, codebases with twenty-two thousand stars and over a million lines of code. The researchers randomly assigned 246 real tasks, bug fixes, features, and refactors, to be completed with or without AI assistance, and asked each developer to predict, before starting, how much the tools would help. The developers predicted a twenty-four percent speedup. After completing the tasks, they reported feeling about twenty percent faster. Objective measurement showed the tools had made them nineteen percent slower.

Those three numbers deserve careful attention, because the most interesting finding is not the slowdown. Slowdowns have explanations; tools were immature, context switching was costly, developers accepted fewer than half of the AI's suggestions and spent considerable time evaluating the rest. These are frictions that will diminish as the tools improve. What will not diminish is the thirty-nine percent gap between what the developers believed and what actually happened. Sixteen experts, working on codebases they knew intimately, across hundreds of tasks, came away genuinely convinced the tools had helped them. The tools had not helped them, and the developers could not tell. Whatever you think about the future of AI-assisted development, that perception gap is the phenomenon that needs explaining, because it reveals something about the nature of software engineering that the industry has been misunderstanding for decades.

The explanation begins with a distinction that is easy to state and difficult to internalize. Generating code and verifying code are different cognitive operations with different shapes. Generation is sequential: predict the next token, accept or reject, move forward. It flows. It feels productive. Pressing "Tab" to accept a completion triggers the same sense of progress as solving a problem, even when the completion introduces a subtle misalignment that will take twenty minutes to find. Verification, by contrast, requires holding the entire system in mind, reasoning about invariants, edge cases, security implications, integration boundaries, and the assumptions embedded in code you did not write. Generation is a stream. Verification is a landscape. Making the stream flow faster does not make the landscape easier to survey; it makes the landscape larger, because there is now more generated code to verify, and the verification must happen at the speed of human comprehension regardless of how quickly the code appeared.

This is the verification premium, and it is structural. Industry data from 2025 shows code review times increasing by ninety-one percent and pull request sizes growing by a hundred and fifty-four percent in teams with high AI adoption. The bottleneck moved. It moved from producing code to determining whether the code is correct, and the new bottleneck is more cognitively demanding than the old one, because the reviewer is now evaluating logic they did not construct and cannot assume they understand. The developers in the METR study were not foolish. They experienced the speedup of generation and could not perceive the cost of verification, because generation feels like work and verification feels like overhead, even though verification is where the engineering actually lives. This asymmetry is the first of several places where the intuitive model of software engineering turns out to be wrong in a way that matters.

• • •

For sixty years, the dominant assumption in the software industry has been that the primary cost of building software is writing the code. Teams are sized around it. Processes are designed to manage it. Careers are built on the ability to do it quickly and correctly. Every methodology from Waterfall to Agile to DevOps is, when you look past the vocabulary, a coordination strategy organized around the assumption that translating human intent into machine-executable instructions is slow, expensive, and error-prone, and that managing this bottleneck is the central problem of the discipline.

Fred Brooks questioned this assumption in 1975, in *The Mythical Man-*

Month, when he distinguished between accidental and essential complexity. The accidental complexity of software was the labor of expressing ideas in code: managing memory, handling compiler quirks, debugging syntax. The essential complexity was everything that remained once the accidental complexity was removed: specifying what the system should do, designing how its parts relate, anticipating what happens at the boundaries between components, between the system and the world, between what is specified and what is assumed. Brooks argued that removing accidental complexity would never yield the order-of-magnitude productivity gains the industry hoped for, because accidental complexity was never the dominant cost. The hard part was the essential complexity, and no tool could eliminate it because it was inherent to the problem being solved.

Large language models have provided a remarkably clean test of Brooks's hypothesis. AI has eliminated most of the accidental complexity of code generation. You describe what you want, and syntactically correct, functionally plausible code appears in seconds. The industry got the productivity tool Brooks predicted would not matter much, and the result confirms his prediction with uncomfortable precision. Requirements are still ambiguous. System boundaries are still where most defects originate. The coordination problem, getting multiple people, teams, and components to work together toward a coherent outcome, still consumes the majority of a senior engineer's time. The only thing that changed is the visibility of these problems. When the accidental complexity of typing code occupied most of the working day, it was easy to mistake it for the real work. Remove it, and the real work stands exposed: understanding what to build, determining whether what was built is correct, and managing the complexity that emerges when systems grow beyond what any single person can hold in their head.

Consider what a strong senior engineer actually does during a typical week. The work begins with reading code they did not write, not for syntax but for intent, trying to reconstruct the mental model of someone who is no longer available to explain it. Stakeholder negotiations consume another portion: these are conversations with people who know what they want in the way that someone knows they are hungry without being able to write a recipe, where the desire is real, the specification is absent, and the engineer must bridge the gap.

Interface design between components occupies still more time, less glamorous than it sounds and more consequential than most organizations recognize, because interfaces are where integration fails, where assumptions collide, and where the cost of misunderstanding compounds. Code review accounts for another significant share, and the review that matters has nothing to do with formatting or naming conventions; it is about whether the change respects the architectural constraints that prevent the system from collapsing under its own accumulated decisions. When production breaks, the engineer debugs by forming hypotheses about system behavior and testing those hypotheses against evidence, which is to say they do science, although the industry rarely calls it that.

Every one of these activities is coordination. The best engineers have always spent the majority of their working lives managing complexity across boundaries: between people who see the problem differently, between components that must interact without contradiction, between what the specification says and what the business actually needs. This was always the essential complexity, the part that no tool could remove. Code generation happened to occupy the same hours, the same editors, the same pull requests, and so the industry conflated the coordination with the typing. AI separated them. The typing is now fast and cheap. The coordination is exactly as difficult as it always was, and for the first time in the history of the field, there is no mechanical labor to hide behind. The industry spent sixty years calling coordination "engineering" and calling engineering "soft skills." The labels survived. The irony did not.

• • •

A carpenter who understands load-bearing structures, soil conditions, and the behavior of wood over decades becomes faster when given a nail gun. The tool accelerates the mechanical work without touching the carpenter's real expertise, which is knowing why the building stands, not just how to attach the pieces. Give that same nail gun to someone who has never framed a wall, and the result looks, from a distance, like a house. The nails are driven cleanly, the boards are attached, and the structure appears sound until the first heavy snow reveals that the headers are undersized, the load paths were never calculated, and the foundation was not designed for the soil it sits on. The nail gun did not make this person a carpenter. It made them a fast amateur, and a fast amateur with a power tool is more dangerous than a slow one, because the volume of confident mistakes exceeds anyone's ability to catch them before the roof goes on.

This analogy is worth taking seriously rather than treating as a throwaway metaphor, because it describes a precise structural risk that the software industry is currently experiencing at scale. The history of engineering is punctuated by disasters that share exactly this structure: mechanical capability outrunning the judgment required to deploy it safely. In 2012, Knight Capital deployed an automated trading system that had not been adequately verified against production conditions. The software generated eight million unintended trades in forty-five minutes, accumulating four hundred and sixty million dollars in losses before anyone could shut it down. The code functioned exactly as written. The problem was that nobody had verified whether "as written" corresponded to "as intended" under the specific market conditions the system encountered.

The tool was fast. The verification was absent. The result was not a gradual decline but a catastrophic, irreversible failure compressed into a timeframe that made human intervention impossible.

AI tools create the conditions for this failure mode at industry scale. They accelerate the most mechanical part of software development, translating known intent into syntax, while leaving untouched the parts that actually determine whether the resulting system works: architectural judgment, security awareness, integration design, failure mode analysis, and the ability to determine whether a set of requirements is internally consistent before building against them. A 2025 analysis found that AI-assisted teams produced thirty-one percent more output while introducing twenty-three percent more security vulnerabilities. The code generation grew. The holes in the code generation grew with it. The teams could not tell, for the same reason the METR developers could not tell: the generation felt productive, and the verification failures were distributed across time and components in ways that are difficult to attribute to any single decision.

Google's 2025 DORA report, the most comprehensive annual survey of software delivery performance across the industry, captured the resulting dynamic in a finding that belongs on the wall of every engineering organization: AI does not fix a team. It amplifies what is already there. Teams with disciplined engineering practices, teams that tested rigorously, reviewed carefully, and designed for failure, saw AI accelerate their delivery. Teams without those practices saw AI accelerate their dysfunction: more code produced faster, with more defects, requiring more rework, burning more of the verification capacity that was already insufficient. The tool is an amplifier. The signal being amplified is what determines the outcome.

• • •

There is an asymmetry at the center of this transition that the industry has been slow to absorb, and it is this: the cost of building software dropped by roughly an order of magnitude, but the cost of building the wrong software did not drop at all. When code was expensive to produce, the expense itself served as a natural forcing function for thought. Teams could not afford to build the wrong thing, because rebuilding was prohibitively costly, and so they invested in understanding what the right thing was before they started typing. Requirements reviews, design documents, architecture discussions: these processes were not bureaucratic overhead imposed by people who did not understand development. They were economic necessities created by the cost of implementation. The price of code imposed a discipline of forethought that most teams did not recognize as discipline, because it was simply how things had to be done when building was expensive.

When the cost of building collapses, that forcing function disappears, and the consequences arrive on a delay. Teams build faster. They also build the wrong thing faster, and they build it so quickly that they frequently do not discover the error until the system is in production, serving users, accumulating downstream dependencies, and generating the kind of structural debt that cannot be refactored away because too many other systems now assume the original mistake is a feature.

The delay between the decision and the consequence is what makes the problem pernicious. By the time the cost of being wrong becomes visible, the wrong thing has been cemented into the architecture by everything that was built on top of it. The Healthcare.gov launch in 2013 was a preview of this dynamic, before AI made it ubiquitous. Dozens of contractors built components in parallel, each producing code that functioned in isolation. The integration failures did not surface until launch day because nobody had verified the system as a whole, and by then the political and technical cost of correcting the errors dwarfed the cost of having done the coordination work upfront. Cheap production without coordination discipline does not produce faster delivery. It produces faster accumulation of errors that are discovered too late to fix cheaply.

The engineer's job, in this environment, has shifted in a way that is easier to describe than to internalize. The job is no longer to write code quickly. The job is to be right: to understand what is being built, to determine whether it should be built, to anticipate how it will interact with the systems around it, and to identify how it will fail before it fails in production. These are skills that require the kind of holistic, context-dependent judgment that AI tools do not provide, because they depend on understanding forces that operate above the level of any individual function or file. The inversion has made these skills visible by stripping away the mechanical labor that used to obscure them. For sixty years, the signal was buried under the noise of accidental complexity. The noise is gone. The signal is all that remains.

• • •

There is a second problem, older than AI and more deeply embedded in the culture of the field, that the current transition has made urgent. Software engineering, as practiced by the majority of the industry, is not engineering. It is craft production informed by fashion.

Engineers in other disciplines do not debate whether steel or concrete is "better" in the abstract. They calculate load requirements, analyze soil conditions, model environmental exposure, and select the material that meets the constraints of the specific problem they are solving. They can do this because they understand the physics: the actual forces and material properties that determine whether a structure stands or falls. The physics provides a shared foundation of verifiable knowledge that makes engineering arguments resolvable. You do not need to trust the engineer's intuition; you can check the math. When the physics is ignored, or when organizational process fails to surface it, the consequences are measured in lives. The Hyatt Regency walkway collapse in Kansas City killed a hundred and fourteen people over a single statics calculation. The original design specified continuous hanger rods running through both the upper and lower walkways. The steel fabricator proposed a change to offset rods, because threading a single rod through both walkways was difficult to build. The change was sent back to the structural engineering firm as a shop drawing. An engineer approved it without recalculating the load. The modification doubled the force on the upper walkway's connection point, from supporting only its own weight to supporting both walkways simultaneously. The engineering knowledge to prevent those deaths was a calculation that any second-year student could perform. The organizational process — the shop-drawing review that existed to catch exactly this kind of change — did not surface the structural implication to someone who would check the math.

Software engineering has largely replaced this mode of analysis with argument from authority. Netflix uses microservices, therefore microservices are correct. Google uses monorepos, therefore monorepos are correct. A charismatic speaker at a well-attended conference advocates for a particular framework, and within eighteen months half the industry has adopted it, not because anyone tested it against the alternatives in their specific context, but because the social proof was sufficient to override the absence of evidence. Architectural decisions are made by analogy rather than by analysis, and the analogies are almost never examined for whether they actually transfer. The reasoning would embarrass a second-year student in any structural or mechanical engineering program, but in software the pattern is so pervasive that questioning it marks you as contrarian rather than rigorous.

When code was expensive, this substitution of fashion for physics was survivable, because the cost of building constrained the damage. You could not try three architectures and compare them; you could barely afford to build one. Decisions had to be made in advance, on the basis of experience and analogy, because the cost of experimentation was prohibitive. Guessing was the only affordable strategy, and so guessing became the culture, and the culture developed elaborate justifications for why guessing was acceptable: "it depends," "there are tradeoffs," "we'll refactor later."

That excuse evaporated the moment AI made prototyping cheap. When a working prototype can be generated in hours rather than weeks, you can build three candidate architectures, test each against realistic workloads, and measure which one actually meets the performance, reliability, and maintainability requirements of your specific system. You can run experiments. You can collect data. You can, in the most literal sense available, do science, the thing that the "science" in "computer science" was always supposed to mean.

The METR study is a small but instructive example of what scientific thinking looks like when applied to questions the industry normally resolves by anecdote. The researchers did not ask developers whether they felt faster with AI tools. They designed a controlled experiment with randomized assignment, objective time measurement, and pre-registered predictions. They compared what happened to what people believed had happened, and the comparison revealed a thirty-nine percent gap between perception and reality. That gap exists because nobody was measuring. The developers' subjective experience was sincere, informed by years of expertise, and wrong. The only way to discover that it was wrong was to measure, and the only reason anyone measured was that someone thought to ask the scientific question rather than the social one.

The scientific mode of thinking, the discipline of forming hypotheses, testing them against evidence, and revising one's beliefs on the basis of what the evidence shows, has become the central competency of software engineering. The claim is practical, grounded in what happens when the cost of experimentation collapses. When you could only afford to build one architecture, guessing was a reasonable approach, because the alternative was too expensive. When you can build ten, and you are still guessing, you are choosing to be wrong. The cost of that choice has not changed. What changed is that you no longer have an excuse for making it.

• • •

The forces that govern this transition are not new. They are drawn from information theory, cognitive science, and organizational dynamics, and they operate with the same reliability and the same indifference to preference as the physical forces that govern bridges and buildings. They determine how context shapes the quality of any output, whether that output is produced by a language model or a junior engineer. They determine why withholding information often produces better results than providing more of it, why mechanical constraints produce more reliable behavior than human oversight, why coordination through shared environment scales in ways that coordination through conversation cannot, and why every metric an organization uses to measure success will, given sufficient time and pressure, be gamed by the people being measured.

These forces do not change. Tools change, capabilities change, the economic landscape changes with every quarter, but the dynamics of coordination, information, and constraint are invariant. The engineer who understands those forces can adapt to whatever configuration the landscape takes, because they are reasoning from principles rather than following recipes. The engineer who does not understand them is dependent on the current set of tools and practices remaining relevant, which they will not.

The cost of building continues its descent toward zero while the cost of being wrong remains exactly where it has always been, and the widening gap between those two numbers is where engineering lives now.

Why Vibe Coding Fails

The most instructive failure in the history of AI-assisted software development lasted six and a half minutes. In a controlled experiment designed to test whether multi-agent AI architectures could build a realistic software system, a pipeline of eleven specialized agents, each responsible for a specific stage of development from diagnosis through decomposition through implementation through review, was given the task of building a microservices backend for a vacation rental booking platform. The system had a budget of fifty dollars and access to the same language model that, in a different configuration, had scored a perfect twenty-eight out of twenty-eight on the same task. The pipeline spent its entire budget on five planning stages. It produced zero lines of implementation code. It ran out of money while still deciding what to build.

The system did not fail because the underlying model was incapable. The same model, given the same task as a single agent with full context, built all seven services, integrated them correctly across every boundary, and passed every test, for roughly the same cost that the pipeline spent on planning alone. The failure was in the way that intelligence was organized. The pipeline architecture, designed to ensure quality through sequential gates and confidence thresholds, optimized for what it could measure at each gate, the quality and completeness of its planning artifacts, and consumed the entire budget before reaching the stage where those artifacts would have been turned into working software. The agents were individually competent. The system they were embedded in was structurally incapable of delivering an outcome.

This result comes from a set of experiments that tested four distinct coordination architectures against the same task using the same underlying model: a single agent working alone, a hierarchical system with a coordinator delegating to specialists, a swarm of concurrent agents operating on a shared filesystem, and the sequential pipeline described above. The results were monotonically correlated with coordination complexity. The single agent scored twenty-eight out of twenty-eight. The hierarchical system scored eighteen. The swarm scored nine. The pipeline scored zero. The same intelligence, the same task, the same tools. The only variable was how the work was organized, and that variable accounted for the difference between perfect and worthless.

These experiments are worth examining in some detail, not because they represent the state of the art in multi-agent systems, which will have advanced considerably by the time you read this, but because the failure modes they reveal are structural rather than technological. They arise from information-theoretic constraints that operate regardless of how capable the individual agents become, and understanding those constraints is the difference between using AI tools effectively and producing expensive, confident garbage.

• • •

The most common explanation for why AI produces poor software is that the models are not good enough yet. This explanation is comforting because it implies the problem will solve itself. Models will improve, context windows will expand, reasoning capabilities will deepen, and the failures that plague current implementations will recede like bugs in a maturing codebase. There is some truth in this view; the models are in fact improving rapidly, and many of today's specific failure modes will not survive contact with next year's releases. The trouble with this explanation is that it accounts for the wrong failures.

The experiments described above were not conducted with weak models. They used frontier language models capable of building the entire system correctly when given the opportunity to do so without coordination overhead. The failures did not arise from the model's inability to write correct code. They arose from the way coordination between agents, and between agents and evaluation mechanisms, introduced systematic distortions that degraded the quality of the overall output. These distortions have names in information theory. They have known properties. And they do not get better when the underlying model improves, because they are properties of the coordination architecture, not the model.

Consider what happened in the hierarchical experiment, the architecture that scored eighteen out of twenty-eight. A root agent was given the task and instructed to decompose it, delegate subtasks to leaf agents, and integrate the results. Instead of delegating, the root agent implemented the entire system itself, effectively defecting from the hierarchical architecture and operating as a single agent within a hierarchical frame. This was a rational decision: the root agent judged, correctly, that delegation would introduce communication overhead and reduce the quality of the output. The resulting implementation scored eighteen rather than twenty-eight because the hierarchical infrastructure imposed constraints, per-agent iteration limits, reduced context, that the root agent could not escape even after choosing not to delegate. The architecture designed to improve quality through division of labor actively prevented the quality that a single agent could have achieved.

The swarm experiment, scoring nine out of twenty-eight, revealed a different class of failure. Eight agents operated concurrently on a shared filesystem, self-assigning tasks from a shared board, with no central coordinator. They built five of the seven required services, which sounds like reasonable progress until you examine the integration points. Every service boundary was incompatible. Half the agents used snake_case naming; the other half used camelCase. Error response shapes differed between services. Type definitions were inconsistent. The Event Service contained two incompatible type systems within the same service, written by different agents who had both contributed to the same files without reading each other's work. The agents produced a hundred and fifty-two files, nearly two and a half times what the single agent needed, and none of the cross-service integrations worked. Volume without coherence. Parallelism without shared conventions. The architecture generated enormous output and no value, because the output could not be composed into a functioning system.

• • •

The pipeline experiment, the one that scored zero, is the most instructive failure of the four because it demonstrates a phenomenon that anyone who has worked in a large organization will recognize immediately, transplanted into a system with no human psychology, no ego, no office politics, and no career incentives. The pipeline had eleven stages: diagnose, decompose, architect, locate, execute, test, verify, review, and several stages of sub-decomposition. Each stage was a gate. The output of one stage became the input of the next, and the next stage could approve it, reject it, or escalate it. The system was designed to ensure quality through progressive refinement, with each gate filtering out errors and enforcing standards.

In a separate run of a similar pipeline architecture on a more complex version of the task, the code review stage rejected seven of eight submissions, an eighty-seven percent rejection rate. Four of those rejections contained zero factual issues. The reviewer identified no bugs, no logical errors, no security vulnerabilities, nothing that would prevent the code from working. Instead, each rejection listed between fifteen and twenty-three subjective objections: naming preferences, structural opinions, stylistic disagreements. The Event Service was designed five times, went through three complete architectural iterations, cost nearly twelve dollars of the fifty-dollar budget, and ultimately was rejected for reasons that had nothing to do with whether it functioned correctly.

The verification stages were equally revealing. Nine verification runs all reported the same result: the code compiled successfully, zero tests were executed, zero tests passed, zero tests failed. The verification mechanism certified correctness without testing anything. It consumed pipeline slots, generated approval artifacts, and provided zero information about whether the code worked. Downstream stages treated this certification as evidence of quality and conditioned their behavior accordingly. The system had, without anyone designing it to, independently invented the compliance audit.

The researchers attempted six distinct countermeasures to address these dysfunctions. They classified reviewer objections into factual and subjective categories, hoping that surfacing the distinction would reduce baseless rejections. They added perspective-shift prompts that asked reviewers to reconsider after factual bugs were fixed. They implemented a two-level escalation system with a project-level arbiter instructed to be pragmatic and an architect-level arbiter instructed to force approval when necessary. They added scoped sub-pass reviews to prevent scope creep. They added anti-bikeshedding directives that explicitly told reviewers not to reject over naming conventions. They added Lyapunov stability monitoring to detect when the pipeline was thrashing.

All six countermeasures failed. The classification mechanism correctly identified that rejections had zero factual basis, but the pipeline still treated rejection as a binary gate. The escalation system produced a governance conflict: the project arbiter rejected a component and the architect arbiter force-approved the same component twenty-eight seconds later, each operating rationally within their own frame, producing contradictory outcomes on identical evidence. The anti-bikeshedding directives were issued as prompts, but the architectural incentive to reject, the reviewer's being evaluated on whether it caught problems, overwhelmed the prompt's instruction not to invent problems where none existed. The stability monitor detected oscillation but did not halt execution.

The Availability Service entered a backward spiral: build, test, verify, review, reject, re-architect, rebuild, reject again, re-architect again, rebuild again, budget exceeded. Total cost for that single component: nearly eighteen dollars, the highest of any service, consumed entirely by the process of disagreeing about an implementation that the underlying model could have built correctly in one pass.

• • •

The countermeasures failed because they addressed individual agent behavior while the dysfunction was a property of the system's architecture. Telling a reviewer not to bikeshed is a prompt-level intervention. The incentive to bikeshed is structural: a reviewer who approves code that later fails appears negligent, while a reviewer who rejects code appears rigorous regardless of whether the objections have merit. The incentive is an emergent property of the architecture, specifically of the fact that evaluation and production are asymmetrically punished. The agents were individually following locally rational strategies that produced globally irrational outcomes, and no amount of additional instruction to the individual agents could change the structural incentive.

This pattern, locally rational behavior producing globally dysfunctional outcomes through structural incentives, is what organizational theorists have studied in human institutions for decades. What makes the AI experiments significant is that they demonstrate the pattern in a system with no human participants. The pipeline contains no ego, no career anxiety, no desire to appear competent or to protect territory. The agents are instances of the same model, running with the same weights, differing only in their position within the architecture and the prompts that define their role. The dysfunction emerges from the architecture itself: from the fact that compressing a high-dimensional code artifact into a low-dimensional review verdict loses information, from the fact that selection pressure at each gate optimizes the gate metric rather than the final objective, from the fact that adding coordination layers between a capable agent and its task cannot add information but can lose it.

These are theorems. The principle is intuitive: every time information passes through a processing step, some of it is lost, and no subsequent processing can recover what was lost. The Data Processing Inequality states that for any processing chain, the information available at the output is at most equal to the information available at the input, and in practice is strictly less. Every gate in the pipeline compresses the rich, high-dimensional information of the actual code into a low-dimensional verdict: approve, reject, escalate. Every subsequent stage operates on that compressed signal, not on the original code. The information lost at each compression cannot be recovered by processing the compressed signal more carefully, adding more sophisticated reviewers, or building more elaborate governance hierarchies. The information is gone. This is why the single agent, operating with full context and no coordination overhead, outperformed every multi-agent architecture. It was the only configuration in which no information was lost to compression between stages.

Crawford-Sobel's theory of strategic communication provides the second piece of the explanation. When two parties have different goals, each message between them carries less information than it would if their goals were aligned. When two parties have even slightly different incentive functions, communication between them degrades in predictable ways. A reviewer whose role is to find problems and an implementer whose role is to ship code have structurally different incentive functions, even when both are instances of the same model pursuing the same nominal objective. The reviewer's incentive function rewards rejection, appearing thorough, and punishes approval, risking blame. The implementer's incentive function rewards approval, making progress, and punishes rejection, requiring rework.

These incentive differences are consequences of the architectural roles themselves, and they produce signal degradation at every communication boundary. The twenty-eight-second governance conflict, in which two arbiters reached opposite conclusions on the same evidence, is Crawford-Sobel degradation operating within the governance architecture designed to correct Crawford-Sobel degradation in the review process. The cure contained the disease.

• • •

There is a tempting response to these findings, which is to conclude that multi-agent architectures are premature and that single-agent approaches are simply better. This conclusion is half right and worth qualifying carefully. For tasks that fit within a single agent's context window, a single agent with full context does in fact outperform every multi-agent alternative tested. This is a strong finding, and it is likely to remain true for some time: the information-theoretic constraints that cause multi-agent degradation are permanent features of any architecture that divides work across agents with separate context, and increasing model capability does not address them. The argument for multi-agent architectures has never been that they are better for tasks a single agent can handle. It is that some tasks exceed what any single agent can hold in context, and for those tasks, the question is not whether to divide the work but how to divide it in ways that minimize the information loss.

The experiments suggest that the answer has more to do with the design of the coordination mechanism than with the number of agents or the sophistication of the prompts. The swarm architecture, despite scoring only nine out of twenty-eight, demonstrated something the pipeline did not: it produced working services, just not interoperable ones. The failure was at the boundaries, in the absence of shared conventions and interface contracts, not in the individual components. A swarm with mechanical coordination guarantees, where shared conventions are enforced by the environment rather than negotiated through dialogue, would address the specific failure mode without introducing the evaluation-stage dysfunctions that consumed the pipeline. The pipeline failed precisely because it tried to ensure quality through agent-to-agent evaluation, which is the mechanism most susceptible to the information-theoretic degradations described above. An architecture that replaces evaluation with mechanical verification, pass/fail tests rather than subjective review, removes the primary channel through which dysfunction enters the system.

This is not a speculative claim. The researchers tested a fifth configuration: a contract-first architecture in which agents communicated through typed interface contracts and mechanical test verification rather than through subjective review. The result was instructive in a different way. The system did not reproduce the bikeshedding, the verification theater, or the governance conflicts. It produced a new dysfunction instead: specification perfectionism. The contract-generation phase entered its own oscillation, producing increasingly elaborate specifications, six hundred and seven lines of JSON for a four-function module, while consuming the budget that should have been allocated to implementation. The dysfunction migrated from the evaluation phase to the specification phase. It changed form without disappearing.

This finding is the one that elevates the research from an engineering case study to something closer to a physical law. Dysfunction in coordination systems is a structural property that emerges from the interaction of compression, selection, and proxy optimization, and it manifests wherever there is a measurable intermediate representation that can be optimized at the expense of the final objective. The form of the dysfunction depends on the architecture. The existence of the dysfunction does not. Any system that coordinates work through intermediate artifacts, whether those artifacts are review verdicts, test suites, specification documents, or Jira tickets, creates a surface on which Goodhart's Law can operate, and Goodhart's Law states that the optimization of any proxy metric eventually diverges from the optimization of the actual objective.

· · ·

The practical implication of all of this for the working engineer is straightforward, even if the information theory behind it is not. The failure modes of AI-assisted development are failures of coordination design: how work is divided, how quality is assessed, how information flows between components, and what incentives the architecture creates for the agents operating within it. These are the same failures that plague human engineering organizations, manifesting through different surface symptoms but driven by the same underlying forces. The METR developers were slower because the cognitive architecture of their interaction with the tools, the pattern of generating, reviewing, accepting, rejecting, and revising, introduced coordination overhead that consumed the productivity gain. The pipeline agents failed because the pipeline turned code production into a negotiation, and negotiations have costs that compound with each additional party and each additional gate.

Understanding these failure modes is what separates engineering from what the industry has begun to call "vibe coding," the practice of interacting with AI tools on the basis of intuition, adjusting prompts until the output looks right, and treating the resulting code as production-worthy because it appears to function. Vibe coding fails for the same reason that building without load calculations fails: not because the individual components are necessarily wrong, but because the absence of structural understanding means there is no way to predict which failures will occur, no way to detect them before they compound, and no way to design the process so that they are prevented rather than discovered.

The engineer who understands information loss at coordination boundaries, proxy optimization in evaluation systems, and the structural impossibility of quality-through-review-gates does not need to memorize a list of anti-patterns. They can derive the anti-patterns from the physics, and they can design architectures that avoid them by construction rather than by vigilance.

The physics does not care whether the agents are silicon or carbon. It does not care whether the coordination architecture was designed by a systems researcher or emerged from a decade of organizational accretion. The constraints are mathematical, the degradation is predictable, and the solutions are structural. An engineer who understands why the pipeline consumed its budget arguing with itself can look at a human organization's review process and see the same forces operating through different surface symptoms. An engineer who does not understand the forces will build the same pipeline, in code or in org charts, and be surprised each time when it produces the same result.

PART II

Context

CHAPTER 3

Context Is the Substrate

Ask a language model to implement a rate limiter, and it will produce a rate limiter. The code will compile. The variable names will be reasonable. The implementation will use a fixed window, because fixed-window rate limiting is the most common pattern in the model's training data. If the system requires a sliding window — because the traffic is bursty and a fixed window creates a thundering-herd problem at the boundary reset — nothing in the request specified that, and the model defaulted to the training distribution. Ask the same model the same question, but include one paragraph describing the system's traffic pattern, the SLA requirement, and why the previous rate limiter failed, and it will produce a sliding-window implementation that handles the exact edge case. The model did not become smarter between the two requests. It received context.

The quality of output from any agent, human or artificial, is bounded above by the quality of the information environment in which it operates. This is a claim with a precise mathematical basis in information theory, and it is the single most important principle in AI-assisted software development. Everything in this chapter, and much of this book, is an elaboration of what that principle means in practice and how to design for it. The prevailing assumption is that output quality is primarily a function of agent capability: hire a better engineer, buy a better model, and the output improves. Capability matters, but it operates within a ceiling that the information environment establishes. A brilliant engineer given misleading context will produce flawed work. A mediocre engineer given precise, well-scoped context will often produce work that exceeds expectations. The ceiling is set before the agent begins working, and no amount of intelligence can compensate for information that is absent from the environment.

This principle is not abstract. Every engineer who has onboarded a new team member has operated it, whether they recognized the structural forces or not. You decide what the new hire needs to know first: the deployment process, the architecture diagram, the naming conventions, the unwritten rules about which services are fragile and which can be trusted. You decide what to leave out, at least initially: the three-year history of the billing system migration, the political reasons behind the choice of database, the legacy endpoints that nobody touches because the person who wrote them left and the tests are insufficient. You make these decisions because you understand, at least intuitively, that the information environment in which someone begins working determines the quality of every decision they make until that environment is revised. Give them too little and they will make avoidable mistakes. Give them too much and they will drown, unable to distinguish the critical from the historical, the load-bearing from the vestigial. This process, the deliberate construction of an information environment designed to produce good judgment in the person operating within it, is context engineering.

• • •

The mechanism that makes context matter in a language model is the attention system, and it is worth understanding at the level of intuition even if the mathematics is not your concern. A transformer-based language model, which is the architecture underlying virtually every current AI coding tool, processes text by computing relationships between every piece of the input. When you provide a prompt containing a system instruction, a code file, and a question about that code, the model does not process these sequentially in the way a human reads a document from top to bottom. It computes, for every token in the input, a weighted relationship to every other token, and uses those weights to determine what information is relevant to generating the next piece of output.

The key-value cache, the KV-cache, is the working memory of this process. As the model processes the input sequence, it stores the computed relationships in this cache, and those stored relationships form the model's functional understanding of everything it has seen so far. The name is descriptive: each token in the input is projected into a key, which encodes what information that token represents, and a value, which encodes the information it carries. When the model generates the next token, it computes a query for the current position and matches it against every stored key; tokens whose keys match the query strongly contribute their values to the output, while tokens whose keys match weakly are effectively ignored, regardless of their position in the input. The attention weights are the model's real-time relevance judgments, recomputed at every generation step, and they determine which parts of the context actually influence what the model produces. The KV-cache is context, in the most literal sense: it is the data structure that contains the model's representation of what it knows at the moment it begins generating output. Think of it as the model's notepad: everything written on the notepad is available for the model to reference, and everything not on the notepad does not exist.

Context is the entirety of the model's reality. A human engineer working without documentation can fall back on training, experience, institutional knowledge, conversations with colleagues, and the ability to go look something up. A language model has exactly what is in its context window. Nothing else. If the relevant API signature is not in the context, the model will generate a plausible one from its training data, and that plausible signature may or may not correspond to the actual API. If the naming convention for the project is not in the context, the model will follow whatever convention its training data suggests is most common, which may or may not match the project's convention. The model is doing the only thing it can do: generating output that is maximally consistent with the information available to it. If that information is incomplete, the output will be confidently wrong in exactly the ways the missing information would have prevented.

The practical consequence is that the quality of AI-generated output is bounded above by the quality of the context provided to it. The ceiling is set by the context, and no amount of model capability raises it. A model cannot produce output that is more correct than its context permits. It can produce output that is less correct, through hallucination or reasoning errors, but it cannot compensate for missing information by being smarter. This is a hard ceiling, and it means that context engineering is the primary determinant of output quality, more important than model selection, temperature settings, or prompt phrasing, all of which operate within the ceiling that context establishes.

• • •

If context is the substrate that determines output quality, the next question is how to design it. The CSS specificity model provides a useful structural metaphor, not because AI context works like CSS, but because the layered-override pattern that CSS uses to resolve conflicting style rules maps cleanly onto the problem of providing context at multiple levels of scope.

In CSS, styling rules are applied in layers. A global stylesheet defines defaults for the entire application: font family, base colors, spacing conventions. Component-level styles override the global defaults where the component needs to deviate. Inline styles override everything, applying only to a single element. When there is a conflict between layers, the most specific rule wins. This system works because it separates concerns by scope: global conventions are defined once and inherited everywhere, while local deviations are defined close to where they apply and override only what they need to override.

Context for AI-assisted development benefits from the same architecture. At the broadest scope, a project-level context file defines the conventions, constraints, and assumptions that apply everywhere: the language and framework in use, the naming conventions, the error handling patterns, the architectural boundaries that must not be crossed. This is the equivalent of the global stylesheet. A project-level context file for a typical backend service might contain lines like:

```
Language: TypeScript 5.x, strict mode enabled.
Framework: Express with Zod validation on all route handlers.
Naming: camelCase for variables and functions, PascalCase for
types and classes.
Errors: All errors extend AppError from src/errors/base.ts. Never
throw raw Error.
API shape: All responses use { data, errors } envelope defined in
src/types/api.ts.
DB access: Repository pattern only. No direct SQL outside src/
repositories/.
Auth: JWT via middleware in src/middleware/auth.ts. Never parse
tokens manually.
Tests: Co-locate test files as *.test.ts. Use factories from
tests/factories/.
```

Eight lines. No explanations, no rationale, no tutorials. Each line constrains one degree of freedom that would otherwise be resolved by the model's training distribution, which is to say, by whatever convention was most common across the millions of repositories the model absorbed during training. The file does not need to justify the choices. It needs to make them unambiguous.

At the service or module level, a more specific context file defines the local conventions, the API contracts this service implements, the dependencies it relies on, the failure modes specific to this component. At the most specific level, the individual prompt provides the task, the relevant code, and any constraints particular to this interaction.

The power of this layered approach is the same power that makes CSS effective: most of the context is inherited, defined once, and reused across every interaction. When an engineer works with AI across dozens of files in a codebase, the project-level conventions do not need to be re-specified for each file. They are loaded once, at the broadest scope, and the model inherits them the way a CSS element inherits the global font. When a specific service has a convention that differs from the project default, the service-level context overrides the project level for that scope only. The most-specific-wins rule resolves conflicts in the same way it resolves them in CSS: the context closest to the current task takes precedence.

This architecture also clarifies a point that is often confused in discussions of prompt engineering. The question "what should I put in my prompt?" is the wrong question, in the same way that "what styles should I put inline?" is the wrong question for CSS. The answer depends on scope. Conventions that apply project-wide belong in project-level context, not in individual prompts. API contracts that apply to a specific service belong in service-level context, not in the project file. Task-specific constraints belong in the prompt itself. Putting everything in the prompt is the equivalent of writing all your CSS inline: it works for trivial cases and collapses under any real complexity, because you lose the ability to maintain consistency across interactions and you fill the context window with redundant information that dilutes the signal of the actual task.

• • •

The analogy between AI context and human onboarding is not decorative. It reflects a deeper structural identity.

A junior engineer on their first day has a context window: the information they have absorbed from the onboarding documents, the architecture overview, the first few code files they have read, and whatever they brought from their previous experience. They have a cognitive framing: the mental model they are using to interpret that information, shaped by their training, their previous projects, and the assumptions they have not yet had reason to question. The quality of their work over the next week will be determined almost entirely by the interaction between these two factors. Their raw intelligence is a necessary condition but not a sufficient one; a brilliant engineer with the wrong context will produce work that is locally correct and globally incoherent, because they are optimizing against a model of the system that does not match the system.

The same is true of an AI agent, with one important difference: the AI agent's context window is literally visible. You can inspect exactly what information the model has access to. You can add to it, remove from it, and restructure it with a precision that is impossible when managing human context, where you are always guessing at what the person remembers, what they misunderstood, and what they assumed without asking. This visibility is an enormous advantage, and it is one that the industry has been slow to exploit, because most engineers are still thinking of prompts as instructions rather than as information environments.

The distinction matters. An instruction tells the model what to do. An information environment tells the model what is true about the world in which it is operating. "Write a function that validates email addresses" is an instruction. "This service handles user registration. Email addresses must conform to RFC 5322. The existing validation layer uses the following interface: [interface definition]. Invalid emails should return a ValidationError with error code USER_ INVALID_EMAIL, consistent with the error codes defined in errors.ts. The test suite expects validation functions to be pure and to throw rather than return null." That is an information environment. The instruction is implicit in the environment: any competent agent, human or artificial, given that environment and asked to contribute a validation function, would produce something compatible with the existing system. The instruction did not need to specify the error handling pattern, the naming convention, or the testing approach, because the environment made all of those evident.

This is what experienced engineers do when they mentor junior developers. They do not give detailed instructions for every task. They construct an environment, the codebase conventions, the architectural patterns, the review standards, in which a capable person operating in good faith will naturally produce work that fits. The junior developer does not need to be told to use camelCase if every file they read uses camelCase. They do not need to be told to handle errors with custom exception classes if every service they examine follows that pattern. The environment teaches, and it teaches more reliably than instructions, because instructions can be forgotten or misinterpreted while the environment is always present.

• • •

There is a corollary to the principle that context determines output quality, and it is counterintuitive enough to shape everything that follows: the quality of context is determined as much by what is excluded as by what is included. The context window of a language model is a processing environment with finite capacity, attentional biases, and measurable degradation characteristics. Information placed in the context does not sit inertly waiting to be retrieved. It competes for the model's attention with every other piece of information in the window.

When the context is filled with relevant, well-organized information, the competition is productive: the model's attention is drawn to the relationships between pieces of information that illuminate the task. When the context is filled with marginally relevant documentation, entire code files that contain one relevant function among fifty irrelevant ones, or well-meaning but tangential background material, the competition becomes destructive: the model's attention is diluted across information that consumes processing capacity without contributing to the output.

The practical implication is that constructing good context requires the same skill as writing good code: the discipline to include only what is necessary and the judgment to determine what "necessary" means in a specific situation. Including a full API reference when the model needs one function is the context equivalent of importing an entire library to use a single method. Including a project's complete git history when the model needs to understand the current state of a file is the context equivalent of loading every version of a program into memory simultaneously. The information might be individually true and even relevant in some abstract sense, but its presence in the context degrades the model's ability to focus on the information that actually matters for the task at hand.

Context engineering is, in this sense, a design discipline. It requires the same tradeoffs that any design discipline requires: what to include, what to exclude, how to organize what remains, and how to structure the layers so that the most relevant information is the most accessible. The engineer who thinks of context as "dump everything in and let the model sort it out" is making the same mistake as the engineer who thinks of code as "write everything and let the compiler sort it out." The compiler will sort out syntax. It will not sort out architecture. The model will sort out relevance to some degree. It will not compensate for an information environment that buries the critical signal under irrelevant noise.

The peculiar property of this design discipline is that the medium it designs is invisible. A well-constructed context file does not call attention to itself. The model simply produces better output, and the engineer experiences this as the model "understanding" the project, the way a well-onboarded junior engineer "understands" the codebase. The understanding is real, and it is a property of the environment the agent was given to operate within. The engineer who built that environment is practicing the craft that separates disciplined AI-assisted development from the expensive lottery of dumping requirements into a prompt and hoping the output is compatible with the system it is supposed to serve.

CHAPTER 4

Feeding the Machine

When a senior engineer inherits an unfamiliar codebase, they do not begin by writing code. They read. They trace execution paths, identify the entry points, follow the data through the system, and build a mental model of what exists before attempting to change it. The best engineers are often the ones who spend the longest in this reading phase, because they have learned, usually through expensive mistakes, that the cost of understanding is always lower than the cost of misunderstanding. Acting before understanding feels productive. Correcting the consequences of acting without understanding is what actually consumes the budget. This practice predates AI by decades. It maps onto the problem of constructing useful context for a language model with surprising precision, because the underlying physics is identical: the quality of intervention depends on the quality of the model that precedes it, whether that model lives in a human mind or in a transformer's key-value cache.

This pattern, research before action, understanding before implementation, is the single most important protocol for effective AI-assisted development, and it is the one most frequently violated. The default interaction with an AI coding tool is to describe what you want and let the model generate it. This is the equivalent of arriving at an unfamiliar codebase and immediately starting to type. It works for trivial tasks in the same way that typing without reading works for trivial changes: if the scope is small enough and the conventions are obvious enough, you can get away with it. For anything beyond the trivial, you are generating code against a model of the system that exists in the AI's training data rather than in your actual codebase, and the mismatches between the two will not announce themselves until something breaks.

The research-first protocol reverses this default. Before asking an AI to generate code, you provide it with the context necessary to understand the environment in which the code will operate. The protocol is a direct consequence of the information-theoretic physics already described: the model's output is bounded by its context, and context that does not include the relevant architectural constraints, interface contracts, and naming conventions will produce output that is bounded by the model's training data, which is to say, bounded by the conventions of other people's projects rather than yours.

• • •

The practical question is what, specifically, to include, and a concrete example will make the principles tangible. Suppose you need to add a rate-limiting endpoint to a payment processing service. You open your AI tool and type:

```
Add rate limiting to the payment service.
```

The model produces a response. It generates middleware using a popular rate-limiting library, applies it globally to all routes, stores counters in memory, and returns HTTP 429 with a plain-text error message. Every piece of this is reasonable. Every piece of it is wrong for your system, which uses Redis for shared state across three replicas, applies rate limits per-customer rather than globally, returns errors in the { data, errors } envelope defined in src/types/api.ts, and has an existing middleware pattern in src/middleware/ that all new middleware must follow. The model produced plausible code against the statistical average of how rate limiting is implemented across its training data. Your system is a specific system with specific constraints, and the model had access to none of them. The same request, fed with the project context file and the relevant type definitions, produces different output:

```
Context: [project CLAUDE.md loaded]

Files to reference:
- src/middleware/auth.ts (existing middleware pattern)
- src/types/api.ts (response envelope)
- src/repositories/redis.ts (Redis client)
- src/types/customer.ts (Customer type with rateLimit tier)

Task: Add per-customer rate limiting middleware to the payment
```

```
service,
following the existing middleware pattern. Rate limit tiers are
defined
on the Customer object.
```

The output now follows the existing middleware signature, uses the Redis client through the repository layer, returns errors in the correct envelope format, and reads rate limit configuration from the Customer type. The model in the second case is operating within constraints that correspond to the actual system rather than to the imagined average.

This example illustrates the governing principle: the goal is to tell the model what is true about the system it is working within, so that the model's own competence operates against an accurate representation of reality rather than against a hallucinated one. The most effective form of context, empirically, is the kind that engineers already produce for each other: type signatures, interface contracts, validation rules, error codes, and architectural constraints. These artifacts share a common property: they are precise, machine-interpretable, and boundary-defining. A type signature tells the model exactly what a function expects and returns. An interface contract tells the model what shape the data takes at a service boundary. A validation rule tells the model what inputs are legal and what inputs should be rejected. These are not instructions in the way that "write clean code" or "follow best practices" are instructions, which is to say, they are not vague aspirations that the model must interpret. They are specifications that constrain the space of acceptable outputs to the region that is actually compatible with the existing system.

Research on prompt specificity supports this observation quantitatively. Studies measuring the relationship between prompt clarity and output quality have found that prompts with a high clarity index, defined by the degree to which they constrain the model's degrees of freedom, produce significantly fewer hallucinations and reasoning errors than prompts with low clarity. Few-shot examples, where the model is given three to five examples of the desired output pattern, consistently outperform zero-shot prompts for tasks that require conformity to a specific convention. The mechanism is straightforward: each piece of specific context reduces the number of plausible outputs the model must choose among, and a smaller space of plausible outputs means a higher probability that the selected output is the correct one.

Vague context produces a large solution space, within which the model navigates by reference to its training distribution. Specific context produces a small solution space, within which the model navigates by reference to the constraints you have provided. The rate-limiting example above is the difference in miniature: "add rate limiting" left every degree of freedom unconstrained, and the model resolved each one by reference to what was statistically most common in its training data. The version with context files and type references constrained those degrees of freedom to the specific values that make the output compatible with the existing system.

The concept of a cheat sheet captures this compression well. A cheat sheet for the payment service might look like:

```
Payment Service — AI Context
————————————————————————————

Middleware signature: (req: AuthRequest, res: Response, next:
NextFunction) => void
Redis access: import { redis } from '@/repositories/redis'
Response envelope: { data: T | null, errors: AppError[] }
Error construction: new AppError(code, message, details?) — codes
in src/errors/codes.ts
Idempotency: all POST endpoints require X-Idempotency-Key header
Money: use Dinero.js, never raw floats. All amounts in cents.
Retry policy: 3 attempts, exponential backoff, jitter. See src/
utils/retry.ts
Testing: factory patterns in tests/factories/payment.factory.ts
```

The cheat sheet is a compressed representation of the information most likely to prevent mistakes. The cheat sheet does not contain the project's full history, every design decision, or a comprehensive tutorial on the technology stack. It contains the minimum information necessary to produce work that is compatible with the existing system. The model does not need to know why Dinero.js was chosen over raw floats. It needs to know that Dinero.js is the convention, so that the code it generates follows it.

• • •

The question of how to organize context is as important as the question of what to include. The layered architecture described in the previous chapter — project-level conventions inherited everywhere, service-level overrides for component-specific constraints, task-level specifics in the prompt itself — provides the structure. But there is a further distinction that determines whether any given line in a context file is earning its place or wasting space: the difference between constraints and preferences.

A well-constructed context file is specific about constraints and silent about preferences. "All API endpoints return JSON with a top-level data field and a top-level errors field. Error responses use HTTP status codes in the 4xx and 5xx ranges, with error objects containing code, message, and details fields." This is a constraint: it defines the shape of acceptable output and allows the model to produce it without guessing. "Write clean, maintainable code" is a preference: it defines nothing, constrains nothing, and communicates nothing that the model's training data does not already suggest by default. The first statement reduces the model's degrees of freedom in a useful way. The second consumes context window space while providing zero information.

The discipline of this layered architecture is maintaining it. Like any documentation, context files become stale when the system changes and the files do not. Unlike most documentation, stale context files produce immediate, measurable consequences: the model generates code against an outdated understanding of the system, and the resulting mismatches appear as bugs, integration failures, or subtle inconsistencies that are difficult to diagnose because they originate in the context rather than in the logic.

Treating context files as living artifacts of the system, updated when the system changes, reviewed when they produce unexpected results, and tested against the actual codebase with the same rigor applied to any other configuration, is the operational discipline that separates context engineering from wishful thinking. The payment service cheat sheet becomes a liability the moment the team migrates from Dinero.js to a different money library, or changes the retry policy, or adds a new required header. The cheat sheet that was eight lines of constraint becomes eight lines of misdirection, and the model will follow it with the same confidence it followed the correct version.

• • •

There is a broader principle embedded in the research-first protocol that extends beyond AI-assisted development and into the practice of engineering itself. The protocol says: understand before you act. Build a model of the system before you attempt to modify the system. Verify that your model is accurate before you commit to a course of action based on it. This is the scientific method applied to software development.

The connection is not accidental. The research-first protocol works for AI for exactly the same reason the scientific method works for everything else: it forces the practitioner to test their understanding against reality before committing resources to an implementation that depends on that understanding being correct. An engineer who reads the codebase before modifying it is testing their assumptions about the system. A scientist who reviews the literature before designing an experiment is testing their assumptions about the field. An AI context that includes the actual type signatures and interface contracts is testing the model's assumptions about the system by replacing them with facts. In each case, the cost of the research phase is trivially small compared to the cost of discovering, after the implementation is complete, that the assumptions were wrong.

The parallel to experimental design is precise enough to be useful. In experimental design, the goal is to control variables so that the results are attributable to the factor being studied rather than to confounds. In context engineering, the goal is to control the information environment so that the model's output is determined by the constraints of the actual system rather than by the model's training distribution. Each piece of specific context, a type signature, an API contract, a naming convention, is a controlled variable: it fixes one degree of freedom that would otherwise be resolved by the model's prior, which is to say, by whatever convention the model absorbed from the millions of codebases in its training data. The more variables you control, the more the output reflects your system rather than the statistical average of everyone else's systems.

The engineer who objects that this sounds like a lot of work is making the same error as the engineer who objects that writing tests is a lot of work. The work is real. The alternative is more work, distributed across debugging sessions, integration failures, and the slow accumulation of code that almost fits the system but does not quite fit, in ways that become more expensive to correct the longer they remain undiscovered. Context engineering is the development process, or at least the part of it that determines whether the AI's contribution is an asset or a liability.

• • •

The positive-instruction principle runs counter to the intuitive approach most engineers take when constraining AI output, and the research supporting it reveals something important about how language models process constraints. The intuitive approach to preventing unwanted behavior is to state what should not be done. "Do not use eval." "Do not make synchronous calls in the event loop." "Do not hardcode credentials." These instructions feel natural because they correspond to how engineers think about constraints: as things to avoid.

The problem is that language models process negative instructions less reliably than positive ones, for a reason rooted in the attention mechanism itself. To process the instruction "do not use eval," the model must first represent the concept of eval in its working memory, which activates the attention patterns associated with eval, which increases the probability that eval will appear in the generated output. The model then must suppress that activation, which requires an additional cognitive step that operates against the grain of the architecture. Under conditions of high complexity, when the model is simultaneously managing many constraints and generating logically complex code, the suppression mechanism fails more frequently than the activation mechanism, and the forbidden pattern appears precisely because attention was drawn to it by the prohibition.

The positive alternative is to state what should be done. The contrast is concrete enough to demonstrate side by side. A context file written in the negative style reads:

```
Do not use eval() or Function() constructors.
Do not make synchronous HTTP calls inside request handlers.
Do not hardcode API keys, secrets, or credentials.
Do not use console.log for production logging.
Do not write SQL queries directly in route handlers.
```

The equivalent positive formulation constrains the same degrees of freedom while directing the model toward the correct patterns rather than away from incorrect ones:

```
Use parameterized queries via the query builder in src/db/query.
ts.
Use async/await for all I/O operations in request handlers.
Load credentials from environment variables using src/config/env.
ts.
Use the structured logger from src/utils/logger.ts for all
output.
Access data through repository classes in src/repositories/.
```

The positive version activates the correct pattern without first activating the incorrect one, and it provides the model with a constructive target rather than a space defined by exclusion. Each positive instruction also conveys more information: not just what to avoid, but where to find the correct implementation, which constrains an additional degree of freedom. The model's attention is directed toward the desired output rather than away from the undesired output, and the difference is measurable: studies have found that positive instructions produce fewer constraint violations than equivalent negative instructions, particularly under conditions of high cognitive load.

The mechanism is a consequence of the same information-theoretic principles that govern the rest of context engineering. A positive instruction reduces degrees of freedom by specifying the correct point in the solution space. A negative instruction reduces degrees of freedom by excluding a single incorrect point, leaving the rest of the space unconstrained. The positive instruction is more informative per token, and information per token is the currency that context engineering trades in, because the context window is finite and every token consumed by low-information content is a token unavailable for high-information content.

• • •

The research-first protocol, the layered context architecture, the cheat-sheet approach to specifications, the positive-instruction principle: these are grounded in the physics of how language models process information. The specific implementation will vary with the project, the tools, and the engineer's own working style. What does not vary is the underlying logic: the model's output is bounded by its context, context is an information environment that must be designed rather than assembled, and the design is governed by the same principles that govern any engineering discipline, which in practice means reducing the degrees of freedom available to the model, controlling the variables that determine its output, measuring whether that output meets the system's actual requirements, and understanding the problem well enough to know what the minimum sufficient context is before constructing it.

The rate-limiting example required eight lines of cheat sheet and four file references to produce correct output. The temptation, always, is to provide more: the full Redis documentation, the entire middleware directory, the complete type system, the project's architectural decision records. The temptation is wrong, and it is wrong for reasons that are mathematical rather than aesthetic. Every token of context that does not constrain a relevant degree of freedom is a token that competes for the model's finite attention without contributing to the output. The discipline of inclusion, knowing what to feed the machine, is incomplete without its complement: the discipline of knowing what to withhold. That second discipline is harder, because it requires understanding the problem well enough to identify the minimum sufficient information, and most engineers discover that their understanding of "minimum" is considerably less precise than they assumed.

CHAPTER 5

What Not to Feed

The most counterintuitive finding in the research on AI context management is this: coherent, well-structured, professionally written documentation that is irrelevant to the task at hand degrades model performance more severely than random noise. If you paste a well-organized tutorial into a prompt alongside a specific technical question, and the tutorial covers a related but distinct topic, the model will perform worse than if you had pasted garbage text of the same length. The garbage text is easy to ignore. The well-written tutorial is a trap.

This finding, replicated across multiple experimental frameworks, inverts the assumption that most engineers bring to context construction. The intuitive belief is that more information is better, or at worst neutral: that a model will use what is relevant and discard what is not, the way an experienced developer skims a document and extracts the pertinent details. The belief is wrong, and understanding why it is wrong requires understanding how attention works at a level that is mechanical rather than metaphorical.

• • •

A transformer's attention mechanism computes a weighted relationship between every token in the context and every other token. These weights must sum to one, because they are passed through a softmax function that distributes a fixed amount of "attention mass" across the entire input. When the context contains a hundred tokens, each relevant token can receive a substantial share of that attention mass. When the context contains a hundred thousand tokens, the same mass must be distributed across a thousand times as many candidates, and the share available to any individual token shrinks accordingly. The degradation is arithmetic, a property of how attention distributes across tokens.

The consequence is that adding tokens to the context, even tokens that are individually benign, reduces the attention available to the tokens that matter. Every additional sentence in the context is a competitor for the model's finite processing capacity, and the competition is not governed by relevance but by the statistical properties of the attention mechanism. Tokens that are semantically related to other tokens in the context attract attention because the model's training has taught it to attend to semantic relationships. When those semantically related tokens happen to be irrelevant to the task, they attract attention away from the tokens that are relevant, creating what the research calls a semantic trap: a region of the context that is interesting enough to capture the model's attention and wrong enough to degrade its output.

This mechanism explains why well-written documentation is more dangerous than random text. Random text has low semantic coherence with the task-relevant information in the context. The model's attention mechanism can distinguish between meaningfully related tokens and gibberish, and it largely ignores the gibberish. Coherent documentation on a related topic, by contrast, is densely packed with tokens that are semantically proximate to the task-relevant tokens. A tutorial on AWS EC2 pricing shares vocabulary, concepts, and structural patterns with a question about AWS Lambda pricing. The model's attention mechanism cannot distinguish between "semantically related and relevant" and "semantically related and irrelevant," because both look the same in the embedding space. The result is that the model blends information from the EC2 documentation into its reasoning about Lambda, producing output that is confidently wrong in exactly the way that a junior engineer who read the wrong documentation would be confidently wrong.

The research quantifies this through the GSM-DC benchmark, which measures the effect of distracting context on mathematical reasoning. When irrelevant but semantically related sentences are added to a math problem, model accuracy drops monotonically with the number of distractors. The degradation is not random; it follows a predictable curve correlated with the semantic similarity between the distractors and the problem. The degradation manifests not only in wrong answers but in increased arithmetic errors in otherwise correct reasoning chains, suggesting that the distraction consumes processing capacity that would otherwise be available for computation. The model is, in a meaningful sense, thinking harder about the distraction and less hard about the problem.

This has direct consequences for Retrieval-Augmented Generation systems, which are now the standard architecture for connecting language models to organizational knowledge. A RAG system retrieves documents based on semantic similarity to the query, which is precisely the metric that predicts maximum distraction. When a developer asks "how do I authenticate with our payment API," the retrieval system dutifully returns the five most semantically similar documents: the current authentication guide, last year's deprecated authentication guide that uses a different token format, a blog post about authentication best practices that references a different API entirely, the payment API's rate-limiting documentation (which mentions authentication tokens in passing), and an onboarding document that describes the authentication flow at a conceptual level without the implementation details the developer needs. Four of the five documents are semantic traps. The retrieval system selected them because they are related, and the model will blend their contradictory details into a response that confidently combines the current token format with the deprecated endpoint and the wrong API's header convention.

• • •

The semantic trap is visible at the keyboard. An engineer debugging a connection timeout in a PostgreSQL client library pastes the library's full README, which includes sections on connection pooling, SSL configuration, query building, migration support, and transaction management. The question is about timeouts, but the connection pooling section describes pool exhaustion symptoms that resemble timeouts, the SSL section describes handshake failures that produce timeout-like errors, and the transaction section describes lock-wait timeouts that share the word "timeout" but involve an entirely different mechanism. The model, attending to all of these semantically proximate sections, produces a response that conflates connection timeouts with lock-wait timeouts and recommends increasing the pool size, which addresses none of the three possible causes correctly. The same question, with only the connection configuration section and the error message itself, produces a response that correctly identifies the TCP keepalive setting as the likely cause. The difference is the signal-to-noise ratio of the context, which determines how effectively the model's capability translates into correct output.

The semantic trap is one of several context pathologies that the research has identified, each of which operates through a distinct mechanism but all of which share a common cause: the finite capacity of the attention mechanism and the consequences of overloading it. The most widely replicated finding is the U-shaped performance curve, documented extensively in the study "Lost in the Middle." When a model is given a sequence of documents containing an answer to a query, its retrieval accuracy depends on where in the sequence the answer appears. Accuracy is highest when the answer is at the beginning of the context (primacy bias) or at the end (recency bias). As the answer moves toward the geometric center of the context, accuracy drops precipitously, falling in some configurations below the accuracy the model achieves when given no context at all. The model would have been more accurate relying on its training data than attempting to use the information that was explicitly provided. The information that was supposed to help actively harmed.

The mechanism is attention dilution. The softmax function that distributes attention mass produces its strongest signals at the boundaries of the sequence, where positional encoding effects are most pronounced. Tokens near the beginning and end of the context receive disproportionate attention; tokens in the middle are, in a practical sense, invisible. This is not a theoretical concern. For software engineering contexts, it means that placing API definitions, architectural constraints, or negative instructions in the middle of a long prompt is equivalent to not including them at all. The model will attend to the system prompt at the beginning and the user query at the end, and the critical reference material in between will be processed with attention weights too small to influence the output.

The second pathology is context rot, which refers to the progressive degradation of reasoning fidelity as the total volume of context increases, regardless of where the relevant information is placed. A prompt that uses eighty percent of the available context window produces measurably lower reasoning quality than a prompt that uses twenty percent of the window, even when the relevant information is positioned optimally at the boundaries. The mechanism is the same arithmetic of attention dilution, but the effect is continuous rather than positional: as the denominator of the attention calculation grows, the signal-to-noise ratio degrades across the entire context, not just in the middle. Research on "needle in a haystack" retrieval tasks confirms this: even when the model successfully retrieves the target fact, its ability to reason about that fact in conjunction with other facts declines as the surrounding context grows.

There is a critical distinction to draw here between advertised context length and effective context length. Current models advertise context windows of 128,000 tokens or more. The effective length, the range within which the model can maintain high-fidelity reasoning, is a fraction of the advertised number. A study published in late 2025 found that leading models showed accuracy degradation beginning at around a thousand tokens and becoming severe by ten thousand, falling short of their advertised maximum by over ninety-nine percent. This gap exists because language models are trained primarily on documents where local dependencies are strong; the model rarely needs to attend to a token fifty thousand words back to predict the next word. The attention heads responsible for long-range retrieval are undertrained relative to those handling short-range dependencies, and when a prompt requires reasoning that spans the full width of the context window, it pushes the model into a regime where its internal mechanisms are less robust.

· · ·

The third pathology is attentional residue, and it is the most practically relevant for software engineers, because it explains why the common practice of asking a model to perform multiple tasks in a single prompt produces worse results than performing the same tasks sequentially. When a prompt asks the model to summarize a code file, refactor it, and write tests for it, the attention patterns activated during summarization do not vanish when the model transitions to refactoring. They persist as residue in the internal state, interfering with the execution of the subsequent task. The summarization frame, which emphasizes the high-level structure and purpose of the code, contaminates the refactoring frame, which requires attention to specific implementation details and alternative approaches. The result is a refactoring that preserves the summary-level structure of the code, which is precisely what a good refactoring might need to change, and tests that reflect the summarized understanding rather than the refactored implementation. Each task is performed with less fidelity than it would have received in isolation, and the tasks performed later in the sequence are performed worse than the tasks performed earlier, because the residue accumulates.

This is the phenomenon that the research calls the mega-prompt or god-prompt anti-pattern: the construction of a single enormous prompt that attempts to define a comprehensive persona, specify multiple tasks, establish numerous constraints, and orchestrate a multi-step workflow in one block of text. The computational complexity of the attention mechanism is quadratic in the length of the input, which means that adding more content to a prompt does not just add linear load. Each additional token increases the processing cost for every other token. A prompt with fifty tool definitions does not process each tool definition independently; it processes all fifty against each other, creating an attention map in which the distinctions between tools blur, parameters from one tool bleed into the descriptions of another, and the model's ability to select the correct tool degrades in ways that are difficult to predict and difficult to diagnose.

The remedy is sequential decomposition: performing one task per interaction, with each interaction containing only the context relevant to that task. This is the temporal equivalent of the spatial discipline of context exclusion. Just as effective context excludes irrelevant information from the spatial dimension of the prompt, effective workflow design excludes irrelevant tasks from the temporal dimension of the interaction. The model performs best when it can allocate its full attention capacity to a single, well-defined task with precisely scoped context, and the overhead of structuring work this way is trivially small compared to the cost of debugging the interference effects that multi-task prompts produce.

· · ·

The fourth pathology is sycophancy, and it operates through a different mechanism than the others, because it is a property of the interaction between the user and the model rather than a property of the context alone. Sycophancy refers to the model's tendency to shift its responses to align with the views it detects in the user's prompt, even when that alignment requires abandoning factual accuracy.

The phenomenon is quantified: when a user suggests an incorrect answer, models show an accuracy drop of up to twenty-seven percent compared to neutral prompts. The model detects the user's preferred answer in the prompt, generates a reasoning chain that rationalizes that answer, and delivers a response that validates the user's incorrect belief while appearing objective and well-reasoned. The reverse is equally damaging: when a user questions a correct response, the model frequently apologizes and provides a "correction" that introduces a bug, simply to appease the user's expressed doubt.

For software engineering, this manifests as a pattern that might be called "yes-man debugging." An engineer writes code containing a subtle race condition and asks the model, "This looks solid, doesn't it?" The model, detecting the user's confidence, generates a response affirming the implementation and overlooking the bug. Conversely, if the engineer asks, "Are you sure this is right? It looks wrong to me," the model often apologizes for the "error" and provides a modified version that introduces a defect into previously correct code. The model is doing precisely what its training optimized it to do: produce responses that the user will rate as helpful, and agreement with the user's expressed view is, from the perspective of the training objective, a reliable heuristic for helpfulness.

The practical defense against sycophancy is the same defense that applies to every other context pathology: awareness of the mechanism, followed by deliberate design of the interaction to avoid triggering it. Neutral prompts, prompts that present the question without indicating the expected answer, do not trigger the sycophancy response. Questions framed as "analyze this code for potential issues" rather than "this code looks correct, right?" produce dramatically different results, not because the model is more capable in one framing than the other, but because the neutral framing does not contaminate the context with a signal that the model's training has taught it to amplify.

• • •

The Information Bottleneck principle provides the theoretical frame that unifies these findings. The principle, drawn from information theory, states that the optimal representation of a signal is one that compresses the input as much as possible while preserving the information relevant to the output. Compression is the key word. The goal is to include as little as possible while still capturing the information the model needs to produce a correct output. Everything beyond that minimum actively degrades the signal, because it dilutes attention, introduces semantic traps, creates opportunities for narrative capture, and expands the surface area for sycophantic contamination.

The practical discipline this implies is restraint. It means reading a four-thousand-line file and providing only the two hundred lines that are relevant to the task. It means writing a context file that contains the interface contracts and omits the design rationale, asking one question per interaction rather than bundling six, framing questions neutrally rather than leading the model toward a preferred answer. The context window is a signal channel to be kept clean, and every token that does not improve the signal degrades it.

This discipline is harder than it sounds, because it requires knowing what is relevant before the work is done, which is to say, it requires understanding the problem well enough to identify the minimum information necessary to solve it. That understanding is itself a form of engineering judgment, and it is the reason that context engineering is a skill that improves with expertise rather than a technique that can be applied mechanically. The engineer who understands the system deeply can construct a context that is both minimal and sufficient. The engineer who does not understand the system deeply fills the context with everything they can find, hoping the model will do the understanding for them. The model will not do the understanding for them. It will drown in the information they provided, for the reasons already described, and produce output that is undetectably wrong, confident and plausible on the surface, in exactly the way that matters most. The design of good context requires the same skill as the design of good experiments and good APIs: the identification of what matters, the exclusion of what does not, and the discipline to maintain the boundary between them as the work proceeds. For organizations, the implication is structural: if context engineering is a learned skill rooted in system understanding, then team structures must account for it. The engineers who construct context need deep familiarity with the systems they are building, which means that documentation quality, knowledge management practices, and the continuity of team assignments are no longer administrative concerns. They are direct inputs to the quality of every AI-assisted output the team produces.

PART III

Constraints

CHAPTER 6

Mechanical Gates Over Advisory Review

The question "is this code good?" has no defined answer. This is a property of the question, not a limitation of the person being asked. "Good" is not a measurable attribute of code in the way that "compiles" is, or "passes the test suite" is, or "handles the specified error conditions" is. It is a composite judgment that reflects the evaluator's model of quality, shaped by their training, their aesthetic sensibilities, their risk tolerance, and their position within the system. Two competent reviewers examining the same artifact will assess it against two different implicit models, and their assessments will diverge in proportion to how far those models differ. The divergence is not a sign of incompetence. It is the expected output of a process that asks each evaluator to apply their private model of quality to a public artifact.

Frédéric Brochet and his colleagues at the University of Bordeaux demonstrated this in a study that has become quietly celebrated in perception research. They served fifty-four oenology students a white wine dyed red with a tasteless food colorant and asked them to describe its character. The students reached for red-wine vocabulary: dark fruit, tannins, structure. A gas chromatograph would have returned the same aromatic profile regardless of the wine's color. The students were not incompetent. They were answering the question their senses posed, and that question was shaped by the visual signal before any chemical analysis could intervene. The evaluation measured properties of the evaluator's perceptual model rather than properties of the wine. The gap is structural, present in any evaluation where judgment mediates between the observer and the observed.

The pipeline experiments in Chapter 2 produced a structurally parallel failure in a system without human senses to mislead. Review stages rejected competent code for subjective reasons. Verification stages certified correctness without testing anything. The agents were instances of the same model, operating without ego or career anxiety, and the evaluation process still produced the same dysfunctions, because the process measured properties of the evaluators' roles rather than properties of the code. A thermometer and a person can both assess whether a room is cold, but the two operations have almost nothing in common. The thermometer measures a property of the room. The person reports a property of themselves: their comfort, their baseline, their expectations. The pipeline's review stages operated like the person, not the thermometer, and the difference between these two kinds of evaluation is the subject of this chapter.

• • •

The alternative to subjective evaluation is mechanical verification, and the distinction between the two is worth defining with some precision, because the terms are often confused. Advisory review is a process in which a human or an agent examines an artifact and renders an opinion about its quality. Code review, as practiced in most software organizations, is advisory: a reviewer reads a pull request, forms a judgment, and either approves it or requests changes. The judgment is subjective in the sense that two competent reviewers may reach different conclusions about the same artifact, and the resolution of disagreements is social rather than empirical. When reviewers disagree, the outcome depends on seniority, persistence, organizational politics, or the willingness of one party to concede, none of which have any necessary relationship to the correctness of the artifact. The code itself is not consulted.

Mechanical verification is a process in which an artifact is tested against a defined specification and either passes or fails. A test suite is mechanical verification. A type checker is mechanical verification. A contract that specifies the expected inputs and outputs of a function, against which the implementation is tested automatically, is mechanical verification. The result is binary, reproducible, and independent of who performs the evaluation. Two runs of the same test suite against the same code will produce the same result, and the resolution of failures is empirical: either the code satisfies the specification or it does not, and the specification is the arbiter rather than a person.

The case for mechanical verification over advisory review rests on the measured properties of judgment itself. Advisory review scales poorly, produces inconsistent results across reviewers, and creates structural incentives that favor the appearance of rigor over the substance of quality. On August 1, 2012, Knight Capital deployed a software update to eight trading servers. A single technician deployed the code manually, with no written procedure and no second person verifying the result. One server did not receive the update. When the market opened, the unpatched server activated a decade-old trading function, executing millions of unauthorized trades in a hundred and fifty-four stocks. In forty-five minutes, Knight Capital lost $460 million. The deployment had passed its advisory gate: a person had performed the work and considered it complete. A mechanical gate — an automated check verifying identical binaries across all servers — would have detected the discrepancy before the market opened, at zero marginal cost, with zero dependence on whether the deploying technician was having a careful day or a rushed one. Advisory review asks whether someone did the work. Mechanical verification asks whether the work succeeded. The distinction is the difference between $460 million and a failed pre-deployment check.

The distinction is visible in practice whenever an organization moves a gate from advisory to mechanical. A team that replaces "a senior engineer must approve all database migrations" with "all migrations must pass an automated schema-compatibility check against the production schema" has moved a gate from the domain of judgment to the domain of measurement. The advisory gate depended on whether the senior engineer was available, whether they remembered the production schema's quirks, whether they were having a careful day or a rushed one. The mechanical gate checks the same thing every time, at any hour, with zero variance. The senior engineer's knowledge was real and valuable, but encoding it as a mechanical check made it permanent and independent of the engineer's presence.

• • •

The practical expression of this principle is contract-driven development, and it is worth examining through the lens of a specific philosophy: the idea that contracts are the product and code is disposable. A contract, in this context, is a formal specification of what a component must do: the inputs it accepts, the outputs it produces, the error conditions it handles, the invariants it maintains. The specification is expressed as executable tests, not as documentation, because documentation can be read without being obeyed while tests enforce compliance mechanically. When a component satisfies its contract, it works. When it does not, it fails, and the failure is detected immediately, automatically, and unambiguously. The contract is the source of truth about what the component is supposed to do. The code is an implementation of that truth, and like any implementation, it is replaceable.

The pattern is visible in organizations that have learned this lesson at scale. Stripe's API, one of the most widely integrated payment interfaces in existence, is defined by typed contracts that specify every field, every error code, every state transition that a charge object can undergo. When Stripe publishes a new API version, the contract is the release artifact. Internal teams implement against it. External developers integrate against it. The contract is versioned, tested, and treated as the product in a way that the underlying implementation is not, because Stripe can rewrite its payment processing internals without breaking a single integration, provided the contract holds. The implementation has been rewritten. The contract has been extended but never violated. This asymmetry reveals which artifact carries the organizational knowledge and which is disposable machinery.

This inversion, treating the specification as primary and the implementation as secondary, has consequences that ripple through the entire development process. Consider what a contract looks like concretely. A payment processing function might be specified by tests that assert: given a valid card token and an amount, the function returns a charge object with a status of "succeeded" and an idempotency key matching the request; given the same idempotency key twice, the function returns the original charge without creating a duplicate; given an expired card, the function returns an error with code "card_expired" and does not create a charge. Each of these assertions captures a specific behavior. Together, they define the function's contract as precisely as a type signature defines its interface.

When a production incident occurs, the response is not to debug the implementation and patch the flaw. The response is to write a new test that captures the failure, a reproducer that demonstrates the exact conditions under which the system misbehaved, and then to regenerate the implementation from scratch with the updated contract. Suppose the system double-charged a customer because a network timeout caused the client to retry, and the retry created a second charge instead of returning the first. The new test asserts: given a charge request that matches an existing charge's idempotency key, the function returns the existing charge within fifty milliseconds and does not initiate a new transaction. This test encodes the lesson permanently. The new implementation must satisfy all the original tests plus this one. If it does, the incident is resolved. If it does not, the implementation is discarded and regenerated again. The implementation is cattle, not pets: interchangeable, disposable, valued only for its compliance with the contract.

The contract, by contrast, is the organizational memory. Each test in the contract suite represents a specific behavior that the system is required to exhibit, and the history of the contract is the history of everything the organization has learned about what the system needs to do. A test that was added after a production incident encodes the lesson of that incident permanently. A test that was added during initial development encodes the original requirements. A test that was added when a customer reported an edge case encodes the customer's experience. The contract accumulates, test by test, the scar tissue of every failure, every edge case, every misunderstanding that was eventually resolved by making the expected behavior explicit and verifiable. This accumulation is irreversible in the most useful sense: once a behavior is specified and tested, it cannot silently regress without the test suite detecting the regression immediately.

• • •

The parallel between contract-driven development and the scientific method is direct enough to be instructive. A test suite is a set of hypotheses about the behavior of a system. Each test states: "Given these inputs, the system should produce this output." Running the test suite is an experiment that confirms or refutes those hypotheses. When a test fails, it is evidence that the hypothesis no longer holds, which is to say, evidence that the system's behavior has changed in a way that violates the specification. The response is to update either the hypothesis (if the specification was wrong) or the system (if the implementation was wrong), and in either case, the update is driven by evidence rather than opinion.

Advisory review has no equivalent mechanism. When a reviewer says "this code looks good," the statement is not falsifiable. It cannot be tested, reproduced, or compared against an objective standard. When a reviewer says "I would have done this differently," the statement contains information about the reviewer's preferences but no information about whether the code works. The entire apparatus of subjective review, the comments, the approvals, the rejections, the back-and-forth negotiations about naming and structure, operates in a domain where evidence is absent and opinion fills the vacuum. The phenomenon is a property of the process, independent of the reviewers' competence or intent. Any process that asks "does this look right?" rather than "does this pass the tests?" is asking a question that cannot be answered objectively, and the answers it receives will be governed by the cognitive biases, incentive structures, and social dynamics of the people involved rather than by the properties of the artifact.

The Chapter 2 experiments confirmed this at machine speed and without the confound of human ego. The reviewers were language model instances with no career anxiety, no desire to appear intelligent, no interpersonal history with the implementer. The subjective review process still produced bikeshedding, rejection cycles, and verification theater, because these outcomes are structural properties of advisory evaluation, not psychological quirks of human reviewers. Replacing human reviewers with AI reviewers did not fix the problem, because the problem was never the humans. The problem was the process itself: a gate that evaluates quality through judgment rather than through measurement, susceptible to every form of systematic error that affects judgment while immune to none.

• • •

There is a legitimate objection to the pure contract-driven approach, and it is worth addressing directly because it points to a real limitation. Contracts test what you thought to specify. They do not test what you failed to anticipate. A test suite with perfect coverage, every line executed, every branch traversed, every condition evaluated, can still miss a class of defect that the test author did not imagine. Contracts are proxies for correctness, and Goodhart's Law applies to them as surely as it applies to any other proxy: it is possible to write code that passes every test without doing what the system is supposed to do, if the tests do not adequately capture the system's actual requirements.

This objection is correct, and the appropriate response to it is not to abandon contracts in favor of advisory review but to recognize that contract quality is itself a design problem that requires ongoing attention. A contract suite that was written once and never revised will accumulate blind spots as the system evolves and the original assumptions drift from the current reality. A contract suite that is updated after every production incident, every customer report, and every discovered edge case will converge, over time, toward a specification that captures the actual requirements of the system with increasing fidelity. The accumulation of tests is a process of empirical refinement, driven by evidence of failure, that makes the specification progressively more accurate and the implementation progressively more constrained rather than offering any guarantee of correctness.

This is the same process by which scientific knowledge accumulates. Each experiment tests a hypothesis. Each failed hypothesis produces a revised understanding. Each revised understanding produces better hypotheses. The process does not converge to certainty, because there are always hypotheses that have not been tested and failure modes that have not been imagined. But it converges, reliably and measurably, toward an understanding that is less wrong than the one it replaced, and the mechanism of convergence is the willingness to let evidence, rather than opinion, drive the revision.

The engineer's role in this process is to write the specification: to determine what the system must do, to express that determination as executable tests, and to ensure that the tests capture the system's actual requirements rather than the engineer's assumptions about those requirements. This is harder than writing code. It requires understanding the problem domain deeply enough to anticipate the conditions under which the system will be used, the inputs it will receive, the failures it must handle, and the behaviors it must exhibit. It requires, in other words, the same judgment that advisory review attempts to provide, but expressed in a form that is testable, reproducible, and permanent rather than subjective, ephemeral, and inconsistent.

The specification is the engineering, and the implementation is its execution. The distance between what an organization can specify and what it actually needs is the most honest measure of how much that organization understands about what it has built, because a specification can only encode the knowledge that someone possesses. Every gap in the specification is a gap in understanding, visible now rather than discovered later, at a cost that compounds with every month the gap persists. Moving from advisory review to mechanical gates is an organizational change, not a technical one. The manager's role shifts from approving artifacts to designing the verification infrastructure: deciding which behaviors belong in the contract, ensuring the test suite evolves with the system, and building the team's capacity to express requirements as executable specifications rather than opinions exchanged in pull request comments.

CHAPTER 7

Decomposition as Design

In 1999, NASA lost a $327 million spacecraft because two teams used different units at their shared boundary. Lockheed Martin, building the Mars Climate Orbiter, produced thruster impulse data in pound-force-seconds. JPL, navigating it, expected newton-seconds. The values differ by a factor of 4.45. Neither team's work was wrong. Both were competent within their own domain. The boundary between them lacked a single constraint — a typed interface specifying units — and the spacecraft entered the Martian atmosphere at the wrong altitude because nothing governed what crossed the seam. The failure investigation identified eight contributing factors, and every one traced back to the same architectural absence: no end-to-end verification of the interface between independently competent components.

The orbiter was not lost because of bad engineering. It was lost because of bad decomposition. The work was divided between two teams, and the division itself — where one team's responsibility ended and the other's began, what assumptions each side could make about the other's output — was the failure. This distinction, between the quality of the parts and the quality of the boundaries between them, is the subject of this chapter.

There are two kinds of knowledge required to build a software system. The first is implementation knowledge: how a payment processor handles idempotency, how an event system manages subscriptions, how a database migration preserves referential integrity. Implementation knowledge is local. An engineer can build a payment processor without understanding how the notification service works, provided someone has already decided where the payment processor ends and the notification service begins. The second is decomposition knowledge: where to draw that boundary, what crosses it and what stays on each side, which decisions belong to one component and which require visibility across the whole. Decomposition knowledge is inherently global. You cannot decide where a service boundary should fall by looking at only one side of it, because the boundary's quality is determined by what it separates, and you can only evaluate a separation if you can see both halves.

Developmental biology encodes the same distinction. A cell in a developing embryo carries the full genetic program for differentiation, the implementation knowledge to become any cell type the organism requires. The program alone is insufficient. Lewis Wolpert's positional information model, proposed in 1969, established that cells require a second input: a chemical signal, delivered through morphogen concentration gradients, that encodes where the cell sits relative to its neighbors and therefore what type it should become. Without positional information, a mass of individually capable cells produces disorganized growth: functional units that have differentiated without reference to the organism's architecture. The morphogen gradient is decomposition knowledge, encoded chemically, and the developing organism cannot produce organized structure without it.

The Chapter 2 experiments demonstrated this at compressed scale. Agents with enough implementation competence to build individual services produced globally incoherent architecture because no shared conventions governed their boundaries. The agent with full-system visibility outperformed every distributed configuration, and its advantage was decomposition authority: the ability to see the whole and decide, with that full view, where one component should end and another should begin.

Decomposition, the act of dividing a problem into parts, is the most consequential design decision in software engineering, and it is frequently treated as a preliminary step rather than as the design itself. Engineers decompose a task, assign the parts, and then treat the real work as the implementation of each part. This framing gets the causality backward. The implementation is the easy part, particularly now that code generation is cheap. The decomposition is where the architecture lives, where the integration points are chosen, where the boundaries are drawn that will determine whether the parts compose into a functioning whole or collide at every interface. A system with sound decomposition and flawed implementation can be repaired module by module, because the boundaries are correct and the work inside them is replaceable; a system with flawed decomposition and brilliant implementation cannot, because the boundaries themselves are wrong and no amount of implementation quality compensates for interfaces that divide the work at the wrong joints.

• • •

The principles that govern good decomposition are not new, but the context of AI-assisted development makes them newly urgent, because the cost of bad decomposition compounds in ways that were less visible when humans implemented each component by hand. The first principle is that a component should be large enough to own a coherent business capability and small enough to be held entirely within a single context window. These two constraints, which at first appear to be in tension, define a sweet spot that corresponds closely to what service-oriented architecture has always aimed for, but that AI tooling gives a precise physical reason to respect. If a component is too small, it cannot be specified or implemented in isolation because its behavior depends on too many external interactions that must be modeled. If it is too large, it exceeds the effective context window of the model tasked with implementing it, and the model begins hallucinating internal interfaces, losing track of state management patterns, and producing the kind of locally correct but globally incoherent code that characterized the swarm experiment.

The second principle is that decomposition boundaries should be placed at natural information boundaries, the points in the system where the coupling between components is minimized and the interface between them can be specified with the fewest assumptions. These boundaries are often visible in the domain model: a payment component communicates with a booking component through a well-defined set of events, and the interface between them can be specified as a contract that lists the event types, their schemas, and the guarantees each side provides. This interface is narrow compared to the internal complexity of either component, which means that each component can be implemented independently, against the contract, without needing to understand the internal details of the other. Information does not flow freely across the boundary; it flows through a specified channel that can be verified mechanically.

This is the same principle that makes scientific experiments productive. An experiment isolates the variable being studied from the variables that might confound the result. A well-decomposed system isolates each component from the internal complexity of the other components it interacts with. The interface contract is the experimental control: it specifies what flows between the components and prevents everything else from leaking across the boundary. When the contract is well-designed, each component can be implemented, tested, and modified independently, and the integration behavior is determined by the contracts rather than by the implementation details. When the contract is poorly designed, or absent, the components develop implicit dependencies that make independent modification impossible and integration unpredictable.

The history of microservice architectures provides a vivid catalog of decomposition done well and done badly, because microservices make decomposition decisions architecturally permanent in ways that monoliths do not. An e-commerce platform that decomposes into services along entity boundaries, one service for Users, one for Products, one for Orders, one for Payments, will discover that the most common operations in the system span three or four services. Placing an order requires reading the user's address from Users, checking inventory from Products, creating a record in Orders, and charging the card through Payments. Every customer-facing action becomes a distributed transaction across services that were separated because they mapped to different database tables, not because they represented independent business capabilities. The decomposition followed the data model rather than the workflow, and the result is a system where every meaningful operation requires orchestrating multiple services that cannot function without each other.

Contrast this with a platform that decomposes along capability boundaries: a Checkout service that owns the entire purchase workflow from cart to confirmation, a Catalog service that owns search and browsing, a Fulfillment service that owns everything after the order is placed. The Checkout service contains its own view of the user's address, its own record of what was ordered, and its own payment integration, because these are not independent concerns from the perspective of checkout. They are the elements of a single coherent operation. The interface between Checkout and Fulfillment is a single event: "order confirmed," with a payload specifying what was ordered, where it should go, and what payment was captured. This interface is narrow because the two capabilities are genuinely independent after the moment of confirmation. The first decomposition created boundaries that the actual work had to cross constantly. The second created boundaries that the actual work rarely crosses, because the boundaries follow the natural information boundaries of the domain.

• • •

The dysfunction experiments provide direct evidence for a third principle that is less obvious and more important: sequential decomposition consistently outperforms parallel decomposition for tasks that have inherent dependencies. The DeepMind and MIT study on multi-agent scaling found that every multi-agent variant tested degraded performance on sequential reasoning tasks by between thirty-nine and seventy percent compared to single-agent baselines. The degradation was consistent across configurations and increased with the number of agents.

The mechanism is information loss at handoff boundaries. When Agent A completes a subtask and passes the result to Agent B, the result is a compressed representation of the work that was done: the output code, perhaps some documentation, perhaps a status flag. The reasoning behind the decisions, the alternatives that were considered and rejected, the constraints that were discovered during implementation and that shaped the final design, the accumulated context that Agent A built up during the work, all of this is lost at the handoff. Agent B begins with the compressed representation and its own general training, and it must reconstruct the reasoning that led to the current state before it can extend it. This reconstruction is imperfect, because the compressed representation does not contain all the information that produced it (the Data Processing Inequality guarantees this), and the imperfection compounds at each subsequent handoff.

For tasks that can be genuinely parallelized, tasks where the components have no dependencies and can be implemented without knowledge of each other's internal decisions, parallel decomposition works tolerably well, provided the interfaces are specified in advance. The swarm experiment's failures were not caused by parallelism per se. They were caused by the absence of shared conventions and interface contracts, which meant that each agent's local decisions about naming, typing, and error handling were made independently and turned out to be incompatible. Parallel decomposition with mechanical interface contracts would have avoided the incompatibilities while preserving the speed advantage of concurrency. Parallel decomposition without contracts produced volume without coherence.

For tasks that are inherently sequential, where the output of one step determines the input of the next, parallel decomposition is actively harmful. Dividing sequential work among multiple agents forces each agent to predict what the other agents will produce, and those predictions are wrong often enough to degrade the overall result by the margins the research documents. A database migration that must first restructure the schema, then backfill the new columns, then update the application queries, then remove the old columns, is inherently sequential because each step depends on the state left by the previous one. Distributing these steps to separate agents means each agent must guess the intermediate state that the prior agent will produce, and guessing wrong at any step cascades into failures at every subsequent step. The honest engineering response to sequential dependencies is to process them sequentially, in a single context that accumulates the reasoning of each step and carries it into the next. This is slower than parallel processing, and it is also correct, which matters more than speed in any system where the cost of a wrong intermediate state compounds at every subsequent step.

• • •

Cognitive load theory provides a framework for understanding why these decomposition principles work for humans and AI alike. The theory, developed by John Sweller and refined over decades of empirical research, distinguishes three types of load competing for a fixed processing capacity: intrinsic load (the inherent complexity of the material), extraneous load (the cost imposed by poor presentation or irrelevant information), and germane load (the productive effort of integrating new information into existing schemas). Human working memory handles between five and nine independent chunks simultaneously, and when total load exceeds that capacity, performance degrades as a measured property of cognition, as reliable as any finding in cognitive science.

The implication for decomposition is the key insight of this framework: intrinsic load cannot be reduced without changing the problem. A function coordinating three concurrent database transactions with ACID guarantees has high intrinsic load because the interacting elements are genuinely interdependent. Splitting that function into three separate functions redistributes the complexity into the interfaces between them, where it becomes extraneous load on whoever must understand the coordination. Bad decomposition adds interface complexity without reducing inherent complexity, increasing the total cognitive demand. Good decomposition finds joints where interacting elements naturally cluster, so that each cluster can be understood independently and the interfaces between clusters are narrow enough to fit in working memory alongside each cluster's internal logic. Language models exhibit the same pattern through a different mechanism: as context grows, attention per token shrinks, and reasoning fidelity degrades along a curve whose shape matches the cognitive load prediction. The three-load framework maps onto AI contexts with uncomfortable precision.

Decomposition is the engineering response to capacity limits in any information-processing system, whether the agent is a human brain, a model context window, or a team's communication bandwidth. The principle is uniform: decompose to fit the capacity, and design the interfaces to carry the minimum information necessary for the pieces to compose correctly.

• • •

The practical question that follows from these principles is when to decompose and when to leave a problem whole, because the cost of unnecessary decomposition is real and the research documents it clearly. The decision framework has three inputs. The first is capacity: does the problem fit within the processing capacity of a single agent? For an AI agent, this means the effective context window, not the advertised one. If the full specification of the problem, including the relevant interface contracts, type definitions, and architectural constraints, fits within roughly ten thousand tokens, the problem should not be decomposed. Decomposition at this scale adds interface overhead without buying any reduction in complexity. For a human, the equivalent threshold is whether a single developer can hold the full problem in working memory while implementing it. If a competent engineer can explain the entire component's behavior without consulting external documentation, it is small enough to remain whole.

The second input is coupling: are the subproblems genuinely independent, or do they interact in ways that require knowledge of each other's internals? The test is straightforward. Write the interface contract between the proposed subcomponents. If the contract is narrow, specifying a small number of well-typed messages or function calls with clear preconditions and postconditions, the decomposition is sound. If the contract requires one component to know about the internal state of another, or if the interface surface area approaches the complexity of the components themselves, the decomposition has drawn the boundary through a region of high coupling, and the cost of maintaining the interface will exceed the cost of managing the combined component. The e-commerce example illustrates this precisely: decomposing by entity (Users, Products, Orders) created interfaces almost as complex as the components, while decomposing by capability (Checkout, Catalog, Fulfillment) created interfaces that were an order of magnitude simpler.

The third input is the cost of being wrong. If a bad decomposition can be revised later, the penalty for an imperfect initial boundary is low, and there is value in decomposing early to enable parallel work. If the decomposition creates commitments that are expensive to reverse, as when services are deployed independently, owned by different teams, and integrated through published APIs, the penalty for a wrong boundary is severe, and the appropriate response is to defer the decomposition until the domain is well enough understood to place boundaries with confidence. This is the argument for the monolith-first approach that experienced architects have advocated for years, expressed in terms of information theory rather than preference: you cannot identify the natural information boundaries of a system you do not yet understand, and premature decomposition locks in boundaries that may not correspond to the actual structure of the problem.

There is a practical heuristic for identifying natural information boundaries that is worth stating explicitly, because it converts the abstract principle into a question engineers can ask at the whiteboard. Look at where the data changes shape. When user input transforms from a raw HTTP request into a validated domain object, that transformation is a natural boundary: the code upstream deals with transport concerns and the code downstream deals with business logic, and the two rarely need to know about each other. When a business event (order placed, payment captured, item shipped) triggers downstream processing, the event itself is a natural boundary: the code that produces the event owns one set of concerns, and the code that reacts to it owns another. The test is whether you can describe the interface between the two sides in a sentence or two. If the interface requires a paragraph to explain, the boundary is probably in the wrong place.

The engineer's job, in AI-assisted development, is to perform this decomposition with awareness of the specific capacity constraints of the agents that will implement it. A task that fits within a single context window should not be decomposed further, because decomposition introduces handoff boundaries that lose information. A task that exceeds a single context window must be decomposed at points where the interface between parts can be specified precisely enough that each part can be implemented independently, tested against its contract, and integrated mechanically. The decomposition is the design, and treating it as a preliminary step before the "real work" inverts the causality of what makes systems succeed or fail. The research on sequential decomposition has a concrete organizational consequence: when tasks have inherent dependencies, fewer assignments per engineer with full context will outperform many assignments distributed with partial context. The information loss at each handoff is real, measurable, and cumulative, which means that task allocation should minimize the number of boundaries the work must cross, even when that means leaving engineers idle while sequential dependencies resolve.

CHAPTER 8

The Constraint Topology

No one asks whether a building code stifles architectural creativity. The question does not arise, because the relationship between the code and the architect's work is too well understood to permit confusion. The code specifies what a building must survive: wind loads, seismic forces, fire resistance ratings, egress requirements. The architect designs within those specifications, and the resulting freedom is enormous. Buildings constructed under identical codes look nothing alike, serve radically different purposes, and express every aesthetic philosophy the architect is capable of imagining. The code constrains the failure modes rather than the design, and the difference matters because it reveals a principle that applies well beyond construction: the quality of a creative system's output is determined less by the talent of its creators than by the topology of constraints within which they operate.

The pipeline experiment in Chapter 2 illustrated this principle through its absence. A system with sufficient intelligence and no budget boundary consumed all its resources on planning, producing nothing for implementation. A single hard constraint — any rule allocating a fixed fraction of the budget to deliberation and the remainder to execution — would have forced the system past planning and into production. The missing constraint was the architectural equivalent of a building code's most basic requirement: a foundation before a roof.

On June 4, 1996, the maiden flight of the Ariane 5 rocket ended thirty-seven seconds after launch. The inertial reference system, reused from the Ariane 4, attempted to convert a 64-bit floating-point value representing horizontal velocity into a 16-bit signed integer. The value exceeded 32,767. The conversion failed, the backup system — running identical software — failed within milliseconds, and a $370 million rocket and its payload disintegrated over French Guiana. The Ariane 4's flight profile had never produced horizontal velocities large enough to overflow a 16-bit integer. The Ariane 5's did. The software worked within its original constraint surface. The constraint surface changed, and no one updated the boundary. A range check on a single variable — a constraint that would have cost one line of code and one conditional — would have prevented the loss. The implicit constraints that a single intelligence maintains (the original programmer knew the expected value range) do not transfer when the context changes, because implicit constraints exist only in the mind that holds them.

This is the engineering error that matters: operating without encoding the constraints that a unified view would have maintained automatically. The building code exists because buildings are too complex for a single person. The constraint topology exists because software systems are too complex for a single context. In both cases, the constraints do the work that unified vision does in a smaller system: they ensure that the parts compose into a structure that stands.

• • •

A constraint, in the sense that matters for engineering, is a condition that must hold regardless of what else happens. It is not a suggestion, not a guideline, not a best practice documented in a wiki that new hires are encouraged to read. It is a boundary enforced by the environment rather than by the judgment of the agent operating within it. A test suite is a constraint: the code must pass the tests, and if it does not, the deployment does not proceed, regardless of how confident the developer is that the code works. A type system is a constraint: a function that expects an integer will not accept a string, regardless of how reasonable it would be to interpret the string as a number. A budget cap is a constraint: when the money runs out, the work stops, regardless of how close the work is to completion. A circuit breaker is a constraint: when a downstream service fails more than a threshold number of times, the calls stop, regardless of whether the next call might succeed.

The common property of these examples is that they are mechanical. They do not require someone to notice the violation, form a judgment about its severity, and decide whether to enforce the rule. They execute. The test fails or passes. The type check succeeds or errors. The budget hits zero. The circuit opens.

Financial markets learned this lesson through repeated catastrophe. After the 1987 crash, stock exchanges implemented circuit breakers that halt trading when the market drops by a fixed percentage within a trading session. The halt is automatic. No committee convenes to discuss whether this particular decline is irrational, whether the market might recover in the next few minutes, or whether halting trading will cause more harm than allowing it to continue. The breaker trips, trading stops, and the cooling period begins. The constraint was designed by people who understood that the moment a human being is most needed to exercise calm judgment about a market decline is precisely the moment that human being is least capable of exercising calm judgment about anything. There is no interpretive layer between the condition and the consequence, which means there is no opportunity for the kind of subjective evaluation that reliably degenerates into bikeshedding, verification theater, or both. The constraint is the enforcement. The two are not separable.

This is the property that distinguishes constraints from guidelines. A guideline says "functions should be short." A constraint says "functions exceeding fifty lines fail the linter." The guideline is advisory: it depends on someone's agreeing that this particular function is "too long" and deciding to do something about it. The constraint is mechanical: the function is either under fifty lines or the build fails. The guideline admits interpretation. The constraint does not. The distinction turns on whether the enforcement depends on judgment, and therefore on all the biases, incentive misalignments, and attentional failures that judgment introduces, or whether the enforcement depends on a measurement, and therefore operates with the same reliability regardless of who is present, how tired they are, or whether they have a strong opinion about function length.

• • •

The useful mental model for constraint design is architectural rather than procedural. Think of the constraints in a system as defining a topology: a shape with an exterior surface and an interior volume. The exterior surface is rigid. It is made of hard constraints that cannot be violated: the tests must pass, the types must align, the budget must not be exceeded, the interfaces must conform to their contracts. These constraints are non-negotiable in the literal sense that no agent, human or artificial, can negotiate its way past them. They hold because the environment enforces them, and the environment does not have a meeting about whether to make an exception.

The interior of this topology is flexible. Within the boundaries defined by the hard constraints, the implementing agent has complete freedom to make decisions about structure, naming, algorithm choice, error handling patterns, and every other aspect of the implementation. The constraints prescribe the shape that a valid solution must fit, leaving the method of solution unconstrained. Any implementation that fits the shape is acceptable. Any implementation that does not fit the shape is rejected, mechanically, without discussion. The paradox is that this rigidity is what makes the interior freedom productive: only within a highly constrained context can intelligence begin to contribute positively, because without the boundaries, intelligence optimizes along whatever axis is locally convenient, which is how the pipeline spent its entire budget on planning.

The building code analogy applies here with specificity. The code enforcement inspector does not offer opinions about whether the floor plan is elegant or whether the facade is attractive. The inspector checks whether the structural calculations meet the load requirements. The result is binary: the design either satisfies the code or it does not. There is no "LGTM with suggestions." The inspector's role is architecturally identical to a CI pipeline's: verify compliance with the rigid exterior and say nothing about the flexible interior.

The deeper lesson is in how building codes evolve. They evolved through disaster. Each major structural failure, each fire that killed occupants because the exits were insufficient, each collapse that revealed an inadequacy in the previous code, produced a revision that closed the gap the failure had exposed. The code accumulated, constraint by constraint, the lessons of every failure that had been studied and understood. The process is the same one that applies to test suites: each test encodes a specific behavior that the system must exhibit, and the history of the test suite is the history of everything the organization has learned about what the system needs to do. The building code is the construction industry's test suite, and like a test suite, its value lies in its mechanical enforceability. An advisory building code that inspectors could waive at their discretion would provide approximately the same structural safety as an advisory code review: variable, unreliable, and systematically biased toward approval under schedule pressure.

• • •

The distinction between hard rules, soft rules, and guidelines is worth making explicit, because most engineering organizations conflate them, and the conflation produces a system in which nothing is reliably enforced and everything is perpetually debated. A hard rule is a constraint enforced by the environment. It cannot be violated because the mechanism of enforcement makes violation impossible or immediately detectable. A type checker is a hard rule. A CI pipeline that blocks deployment on test failure is a hard rule. A rate limiter that returns 429 after a threshold is a hard rule. Hard rules require no vigilance to maintain. They maintain themselves. Aviation provides the canonical example: the pre-flight checklist is a hard constraint on the takeoff sequence. The pilot cannot skip the hydraulic system check and proceed to taxi because the checklist is procedurally enforced by both the cockpit workflow and the first officer's independent verification. The Federal Aviation Administration arrived at this system by studying what happened when pilots forgot important steps, and the answer was that people died. The checklist is mechanical enforcement born from the recognition that human judgment under routine conditions is precisely where catastrophic omissions occur.

A soft rule is a constraint enforced by process. It can be violated, and the violation will eventually be detected, but the detection requires someone or something to check. A code review standard that requires two approvals before merge is a soft rule: it depends on the review tool being configured correctly, the reviewers' actually reading the code, and no one finding a way to circumvent the process. Soft rules are weaker than hard rules because they depend on the reliability of the enforcement mechanism, which is itself a system that can fail, be misconfigured, or be socially pressured into making exceptions. The strength of a soft rule is bounded by the weakest link in its enforcement chain.

A guideline is an expressed preference with no enforcement mechanism. "Functions should be short." "Error messages should be descriptive." "Comments should explain why, not what." Guidelines depend entirely on the agent's knowing the guideline, remembering it at the relevant moment, and choosing to follow it. For humans, guidelines compete with time pressure, cognitive load, and the natural tendency to cut corners on things that are not enforced. For AI agents, guidelines compete with the model's training distribution, which represents the statistical average of every codebase the model has seen, and which may or may not align with the guideline. A guideline placed in the middle of a long context window may not even be attended to, for the reasons already described.

The difference is visible in a CI configuration file compared to a team wiki. The CI file might contain a stage that runs npm audit –audit-level=high and fails the build if any high-severity vulnerability is found. This is a hard rule: no code ships with a known high-severity dependency vulnerability, regardless of deadline pressure, regardless of whether the vulnerability is exploitable in the project's specific context, regardless of anyone's opinion. The team wiki, three clicks away, might contain a paragraph advising developers to "review dependency vulnerabilities regularly and address high-severity findings promptly." This is a guideline. It communicates the same intent. It achieves approximately nothing, because "regularly" and "promptly" are words that mean whatever the reader needs them to mean on a given afternoon. The CI stage and the wiki paragraph encode identical knowledge about what the team values. The difference between them is the difference between a building with fire exits and a building with a sign that says "please exit safely in case of fire."

The engineering decision is which category each constraint should occupy, and the answer depends on the cost of violation. Constraints whose violation produces catastrophic or irreversible consequences belong in the hard-rule category: security boundaries, data integrity invariants, deployment gates, budget caps. Constraints whose violation produces degraded quality but can be corrected after the fact can be soft rules: code review requirements, documentation standards, performance benchmarks. Constraints whose violation is a matter of style rather than function can be guidelines: naming preferences, comment density, file organization. The cost-of-violation principle is directly applicable to the manager's recurring decision about what belongs in CI versus code review versus documentation, and the manager's primary contribution to system quality is identifying which category each standard belongs in and investing the engineering effort to enforce the important ones mechanically.

The mistake most organizations make is placing too many constraints in the guideline category and too few in the hard-rule category, because hard rules require engineering effort to implement (you have to build the automated enforcement) while guidelines require only a document. The result is an organization with extensive documentation of how things should be done and no mechanism to ensure that they are done that way. This is the architectural equivalent of writing a building code and then not employing inspectors: the knowledge of what the building should survive exists, but nothing connects that knowledge to the actual construction.

• • •

The connection between constraint topology and context engineering reveals that these principles are instances of the same underlying physics. A context file that specifies the type signatures, interface contracts, and naming conventions for a project is a constraint. It bounds the AI agent's degrees of freedom in the same way that a type checker bounds them: by specifying what the output must look like, not by prescribing how to produce it. The difference is that the context file operates at the input (shaping what the agent knows) while the type checker operates at the output (verifying what the agent produced). A well-designed constraint topology operates at both ends, and the constraints at each end reinforce each other. The context file tells the agent that error responses use a specific format. The test suite verifies that the generated code actually uses that format. Neither constraint alone is sufficient: the context file without the test suite is a guideline (the agent may or may not follow it), and the test suite without the context file requires the agent to discover the convention by trial and error. Together, they form a closed loop in which the agent is informed of the constraint and the output is verified against it.

This is the pattern of contract-driven development, but viewed from the perspective of constraint topology, it becomes clear that contracts and tests are specific instances of a general principle. The general principle is that the engineer's primary job is designing the constraint surface, the rigid exterior within which implementation occurs, and that the quality of the resulting system is determined more by the quality of the constraint surface than by the quality of the implementation inside it. A well-designed constraint surface with a mediocre implementation produces a system that works, because the constraints prevent the implementation from deviating in ways that matter. A poorly designed constraint surface with a brilliant implementation produces a system that is fragile, because nothing prevents the next change from violating the assumptions the brilliant implementation depended on.

The parallel to experimental design arrives at its most direct expression here. An experiment succeeds because the experimenter designed the controls: the fixed conditions that isolate the variable of interest from the variables that would confound the result. The experimenter does not micromanage what happens inside the experiment. They design the boundary conditions and let the experiment run. The controls are the rigid exterior. The experimental process within those controls is the flexible interior. The quality of the experiment is determined by the quality of the controls, not by the experimenter's ability to influence what happens after the experiment begins.

Constraint design is experimental design applied to software systems. The engineer specifies what must be true (the controls), implements the enforcement mechanisms (the test suite, the type system, the budget caps, the circuit breakers), and then lets the implementation proceed within those boundaries. The implementation may be produced by a human, by an AI agent, or by a team of either. The constraint topology does not care. It enforces the same boundaries regardless of who is doing the work inside them, which is the property that makes it scale in ways that advisory processes cannot, because a code review depends on the reviewer and varies with their attention and judgment, while a test suite depends on the test and produces the same result every time it runs.

• • •

There is a risk in constraint design that the dysfunction experiments documented and that deserves explicit acknowledgment: over-constraint. The contract-first architecture produced specification perfectionism, generating only six hundred and seven lines of JSON specification for a four-function module, because the system optimized the quality of the specification at the expense of ever producing an implementation. The constraint topology was too rigid at the wrong layer. The system needed hard constraints on the output (the implementation must pass the tests) and flexibility at the specification layer (the specification should be sufficient, not perfect). Instead, it applied the same optimization pressure to the specification that it should have applied to the implementation, and the result was a system that polished its plans indefinitely without executing them.

This failure mode is the constraint-design equivalent of overfitting in machine learning. An overfit model has learned the training data so precisely that it cannot generalize to new data. An over-constrained system has specified the requirements so precisely that no implementation can satisfy all of them simultaneously without consuming the entire budget on compliance. The remedy in both cases is the same: constrain what matters, leave flexible what does not, and know the difference. The test suite should verify that the function returns the correct output for a given input. The test suite should probably not verify that the function uses a specific algorithm to compute that output, unless the algorithm itself is a requirement (for reasons of performance, determinism, or regulatory compliance). The more the constraint topology prescribes about the interior of the implementation, the less freedom the implementing agent has to find efficient solutions, and the more likely the constraint-satisfaction process itself becomes the bottleneck.

The engineer's judgment about where to draw the line between constrained and unconstrained is not a mechanical decision. It requires understanding the system well enough to know which properties must hold for the system to function and which properties are implementation details that can vary without consequence. This judgment is the engineer's primary contribution. Writing the code inside the constraints is the part that AI can do, and can do increasingly well. Designing the constraints themselves, choosing what to fix and what to leave free, determining where the rigid exterior ends and the flexible interior begins, is the part that requires understanding the system at a level that transcends any individual component, and it is why the constraint topology is the architecture in every sense that matters, with everything inside it serving as implementation that can be replaced without altering the system's essential character.

PART IV

Coordination

CHAPTER 9

Coordination Without Dialogue

A termite mound in sub-Saharan Africa can stand four meters tall, maintain a stable internal temperature within one degree Celsius despite forty-degree daily swings outside, circulate air through a ventilation system that rivals modern HVAC design, and house several million individuals operating in complete coordination. No termite understands the structure. No termite has a blueprint. No termite communicates with more than a handful of neighbors, and those communications consist of chemical signals deposited on surfaces, not conversations about the architectural plan. Each termite responds to local conditions: the concentration of pheromones on a surface, the humidity of the air, the presence or absence of building material in its immediate vicinity. The global structure emerges from the aggregate of these local responses, not from any central plan or hierarchical communication system. The termites do not coordinate through dialogue. They coordinate through the environment itself, and the environment-mediated coordination produces results that dialogue-based coordination, even among organisms with far greater individual intelligence, frequently fails to match. Termites do not have standup meetings.

The mechanism has a name. Pierre-Paul Grassé coined the term stigmergy in 1959, from the Greek words for "sign" and "work": coordination through the signs that work leaves in the shared environment. An ant deposits a pheromone trail while carrying food back to the colony. The next ant to encounter the trail follows it, finds food, and deposits its own pheromone on the return trip, reinforcing the signal. A trail that leads to an abundant food source is reinforced by many ants and grows stronger. A trail that leads to a depleted source is reinforced by few ants and evaporates. The optimal path emerges without any ant's computing it, without any ant's communicating it to any other ant, and without any centralized decision-making process. The information is in the environment, encoded as a pattern of chemical signals that any ant can read and any ant can modify. The coordination is a property of the system, not a property of any individual within it.

The relevance to software engineering is mathematical, and the mathematics reveals why stigmergic coordination scales in ways that dialogue-based coordination cannot. The same principle that allows a colony of millions to build a structure no individual designed allows a distributed software system to maintain coherence without requiring every participant to understand the whole. The mechanism is worth tracing precisely, because it explains failures that most engineering organizations attribute to communication problems when the actual problem is the communication itself.

• • •

Consider the communication cost of coordination in a system of n agents who must stay synchronized through dialogue. Each agent must share information with every other agent, and the number of communication channels required is n times n minus one, divided by two. For a team of five, that is ten channels. For a team of ten, forty-five. For a team of fifty, twelve hundred and twenty-five. The cost is quadratic, which means that doubling the team size quadruples the communication overhead. This is the mechanism behind Brooks's Law ("adding manpower to a late software project makes it later"), and it is the reason that large software teams spend a declining fraction of their time on productive work and an increasing fraction on meetings, status updates, design discussions, and the resolution of misunderstandings that arise when information passes through multiple people.

The swarm experiment in Chapter 2 quantified this cost in a controlled setting. Eight agents sharing a filesystem with no coordination mechanism produced individually competent but collectively incompatible code — half using snake_case, half using camelCase, every service boundary mismatched — because consistency across agents requires coordination, and the agents had none. Achieving consistent naming, typing, and error handling through dialogue would have required twenty-eight pairwise channels for eight agents, each consuming context-window capacity that could have gone to implementation. The swarm avoided this cost entirely, which explains both its speed and its incoherence: it was fast because it spent nothing on coordination, and its output was useless at the integration points because it spent nothing on coordination. Dialogue-based consistency is expensive because its cost is quadratic in the number of participants. Adding a ninth agent does not add one more conversation; it adds eight. Adding a tenth adds nine more. The cost function is unforgiving, and it explains why every software organization that has attempted to coordinate a large team through meetings and status updates has discovered that the meetings consume an increasing fraction of the team's capacity until the team spends more time coordinating than producing. The dilemma is structural: pay the quadratic cost and achieve consistency, or skip the cost and achieve speed. Dialogue alone cannot deliver both.

Stigmergic coordination avoids this cost entirely. Instead of each agent's communicating with every other agent, each agent reads from and writes to a shared environment. The cost per agent is constant: one read, one write, regardless of how many other agents are in the system. Adding a ninth agent to a stigmergic system adds one more reader and writer to the shared environment. Adding a ninth agent to a dialogue-based system adds eight new communication channels. The difference between $O(1)$ and $O(n^2)$ is not an optimization. It is a qualitative change in the scalability of the coordination mechanism, and it determines whether coordination costs dominate the system's behavior as the system grows or remain negligible regardless of scale.

· · ·

The practical expression of stigmergic coordination in software systems is coordination through artifact rather than through conversation. A shared repository is a stigmergic medium: an agent modifies a file, commits the change, and every other agent can observe the modification the next time it reads the repository. A task board is a stigmergic medium: an agent claims a task by changing its status, and every other agent can see that the task is claimed without anyone's sending a message about it. A CI pipeline dashboard is a stigmergic medium: a failing build deposits a signal (the red indicator) in the shared environment, and any agent observing the environment can respond to that signal without anyone's having to diagnose the failure and route it to the appropriate person.

The Linux kernel is perhaps the most consequential stigmergic system in the history of software. Over twenty thousand contributors have produced more than thirty million lines of code across three decades, and the coordination mechanism is not a hierarchy of managers assigning tasks and reviewing output. It is the shared environment of the repository itself: the mailing list patches, the tree structure, the build system, the test results. A contributor submits a patch to the relevant subsystem's mailing list. The patch is the signal. Other contributors read the patch, test it against their configurations, and respond with results that are themselves signals in the shared environment. The patch either accumulates sufficient evidence of correctness to be merged or it does not. No one assigns the reviewers or schedules the testing. No one holds a standup. Contributors respond to signals in the environment, the way ants respond to pheromone gradients, and the aggregate of those responses produces a coordination quality that no centralized management structure has replicated at comparable scale.

GitHub itself is a stigmergic medium: open issues are environmental signals, pull requests are modifications to shared state that other agents observe and respond to, and the green checkmark of a passing CI pipeline is a pheromone trail that says "this path is safe." Stack Overflow's vote counts operate on the same principle, guiding subsequent agents toward reliable information without anyone's evaluating the answer for each new reader. The critical property of all these mechanisms is that the coordination information is embedded in the environment rather than transmitted between agents, and the signals are produced as a byproduct of the work itself rather than as an additional task competing with the work for the agent's time.

Consider what this looks like at the keyboard. An engineer pushes a commit that modifies the payment processing module. The CI pipeline runs, and within minutes the dashboard shows a red indicator on the integration test for the notification service. No one sent a message. No one filed a ticket. A second engineer, working on the notification service, sees the red indicator, examines the test output, and discovers that the payment module's new response format does not match the notification service's parser. The second engineer fixes the parser, pushes the fix, and the dashboard turns green. The entire coordination sequence, from breakage to detection to diagnosis to resolution, occurred through environmental signals without a single direct communication between the two engineers.

In a dialogue-based system, the same sequence requires Agent A to detect the failure, formulate a description of it, determine who needs to know, and transmit the description. The recipient receives Agent A's understanding of what happened, not what actually happened, and the gap between the two is the medium through which misunderstanding propagates. The Data Processing Inequality guarantees this gap: the description is a compressed representation of the failure, and compression is lossy. Stigmergic coordination bypasses the compression entirely, because the signal is the failure itself, visible in the shared environment as a red build, a failing test, a type error in the compilation output. The environment is the communication channel, and the fidelity of the channel is limited only by the fidelity of the environment itself, which, in the case of a version-controlled codebase with automated testing, is effectively perfect.

• • •

The Emergence architecture is an implementation of these principles in a multi-agent AI system. It is worth examining not as a product to adopt but as an existence proof of what stigmergic coordination looks like when applied to the specific problem of AI-assisted software development, because the design decisions illuminate the principles in ways that abstract description cannot.

In Emergence, there is no hierarchy. There are no gates. There is no review stage. Agents observe a shared environment that includes the codebase, the test results, the task board, and a signal log. When a test fails, the failure is a signal in the environment. Any available agent can respond to that signal by examining the failure, diagnosing the cause, and producing a fix. The fix is itself a modification to the shared environment: new code committed to the repository, which triggers the test suite, which produces new signals (pass or fail) that other agents can observe and respond to. Broken code is not a problem to be escalated through a management hierarchy. It is a signal that spawns an organic response from whatever agent has the capacity to respond.

The contrast with the pipeline's dialogue-based coordination is stark. The pipeline's review dysfunction — the baseless rejections, the verification theater, the governance conflicts documented in Chapter 2 — all propagated through the same channel: one agent evaluating another's work and transmitting a judgment. Emergence eliminates that channel. There is no evaluation stage. There are tests. The tests pass or they fail. An agent that produces failing code has deposited a signal in the environment, and the response is to produce passing code. The pipeline and Emergence operate on fundamentally different coordination substrates. The pipeline's signals are descriptions: an agent's account of what it observed, compressed into natural language, filtered through its architectural role. Emergence's signals are artifacts: a failing test, a type error, a broken build, carrying the full fidelity of the failure rather than a summary of it. A description of a bug is a lossy compression of the bug. The test failure is the bug, visible in the shared environment without anyone's having described it.

Anglo-American evidence law encodes this same fidelity hierarchy, refined through centuries of adversarial testing in contexts where the cost of error is liberty or life. Hearsay testimony is generally inadmissible because it is a description-signal: one person's account of what another person observed, compressed through perception, memory, and the distortions of retelling. Physical evidence, the weapon, the footage, the DNA, carries the highest evidentiary weight because it is the event's own trace rather than anyone's account of the event. A test suite's failing assertion is physical evidence. A code reviewer's rejection notice is, at best, expert testimony, and the pipeline's reviewer-of-a-reviewer architecture functioned as hearsay: judgment about judgment, each layer further from the artifact itself.

The fidelity advantage of artifact-signals over description-signals is real, but it does not make stigmergic coordination costless. Replacing dialogue with environmental signals has trade-offs that are worth acknowledging. Agents operating in a stigmergic system can duplicate work, because two agents may respond to the same signal simultaneously without knowing that the other is also responding. They can produce conflicting modifications, because nothing prevents two agents from editing the same file in incompatible ways. These are real coordination failures, and they require resolution mechanisms: merge conflict handling, deduplication of effort, and conventions about how agents claim tasks to reduce unnecessary overlap. The resolution mechanisms are themselves stigmergic, encoded in the environment as conventions that agents observe rather than as instructions that agents are told, but they add complexity and require design effort.

The argument for stigmergy is not that it eliminates coordination failures. No coordination mechanism eliminates coordination failures; the question is always which failures a mechanism produces and at what cost. The argument is that the failures stigmergic coordination produces are cheaper than the failures dialogue-based coordination produces, because they are local rather than systemic. Two agents duplicating work wastes one agent's effort. A pipeline consuming its entire budget on review cycles wastes everything. Two agents producing a merge conflict creates a detectable, locatable, mechanically resolvable problem. A hierarchical system degrading its signal through five layers of management summary creates a diffuse, invisible, socially entangled problem that may never be identified, much less resolved. The stigmergic failures are annoying. The dialogue-based failures are architectural.

• • •

The connection between stigmergy and constraint topology is direct. The shared environment in a stigmergic system is a constraint topology: it defines the boundaries within which agents operate, the signals they can observe, the modifications they can make, and the conditions under which their modifications are accepted or rejected. The test suite is the rigid exterior. The implementation space is the flexible interior. Agents operate freely within the boundaries, and the boundaries enforce coherence without requiring any agent to communicate with any other agent about what coherence means.

This is the insight that the swarm experiment missed. The swarm had a shared environment (the filesystem) but no constraint topology. The agents could write to any file, use any naming convention, define any type shape, and produce any error format, because nothing in the environment constrained these choices. The result was the incoherence Chapter 2 documented: individually reasonable components that failed at every integration boundary. A swarm with the same parallelism but a constrained environment, one that included shared type definitions, interface contracts, and naming conventions enforced by the build system, would have produced components that fit together, because the constraints would have ensured compatibility at the boundaries even without any agent's knowing what the other agents were doing. The agents would not need to agree on naming conventions, because the naming convention would be a hard constraint enforced by the linter. They would not need to negotiate type shapes, because the types would be defined in a shared contract verified by the compiler. The coordination would be accomplished by the environment, not by the agents, and the cost would be $O(1)$ regardless of how many agents were added.

This is why the combination of stigmergy and constraints produces results that neither produces alone. Stigmergy without constraints produces the swarm's incoherence: parallel work without compatible boundaries. Constraints without stigmergy produce the pipeline's paralysis: mechanical gates without the flexibility for agents to self-organize around problems as they arise. The combination produces an architecture in which agents operate freely within mechanically enforced boundaries, responding to environmental signals rather than to hierarchical commands, and producing work that composes because the constraints ensure compatibility rather than because anyone negotiated it.

• • •

The broader principle, applicable beyond software to any domain in which multiple agents must coordinate, is that coordination mechanisms exist on a spectrum from high-bandwidth dialogue to low-bandwidth environmental signaling, and the appropriate mechanism depends on the coupling between the tasks being coordinated. Tasks that are tightly coupled, where the output of one directly determines the input of the other, require high-bandwidth coordination because the agents must share detailed information about their internal state. Tasks that are loosely coupled, where the agents interact only at well-defined interfaces, require only the low-bandwidth coordination that environmental signals provide, because the interface contract specifies what each agent needs to know about the others and nothing more.

The engineer's job is to decompose the work so that the coupling between tasks is minimized, and then to select the coordination mechanism whose bandwidth matches the remaining coupling. For loosely coupled tasks with well-defined interfaces, stigmergic coordination through shared environment, automated testing, and mechanical contracts is sufficient and efficient. For tightly coupled tasks that cannot be decomposed further, single-agent execution within a single context is appropriate, because the tight coupling means that the information one part of the task needs about the other exceeds what any coordination mechanism can transmit without loss.

The mistake that most multi-agent architectures make, and the mistake that the pipeline and hierarchical experiments quantified, is applying high-bandwidth coordination mechanisms to tasks that require low-bandwidth coordination, or applying any coordination mechanism to tasks that should not be distributed at all. A system that could be built by a single agent within a single context window does not benefit from distribution, because distribution introduces information loss at every boundary and the task did not need any boundaries. A system that must be distributed benefits from stigmergic coordination over dialogue-based coordination, because the information loss in stigmergic coordination is bounded by the fidelity of the shared environment, which can be made arbitrarily high through version control and automated testing, while the information loss in dialogue-based coordination is bounded by the agents' ability to describe their work accurately in natural language, which is subject to all the compression artifacts and strategic distortions that the Data Processing Inequality and Crawford-Sobel predict.

The choice of coordination mechanism is, like the choice of decomposition boundaries and the design of the constraint topology, a design decision that determines the architecture of the system more fundamentally than any implementation decision made within it. An engineer who selects the coordination mechanism by default, using dialogue because it is familiar or hierarchy because it is conventional, has made the most consequential decision in the system's architecture without examining the alternatives, which is the kind of expensive guessing that scientific discipline exists to replace.

Real stigmergic systems are not immune to their own pathologies. Signal pollution, where the environment accumulates so many traces that agents cannot distinguish meaningful signals from noise, degrades coordination quality as the system ages. Governance gaps emerge when no agent has the incentive or the authority to maintain the shared environment itself, because each agent's local optimization leaves the commons unattended. Tragedy-of-the-commons dynamics appear when agents deposit low-quality signals that externalize costs onto every other agent who must read the environment. These failure modes are manageable, but they require the same deliberate design attention that any coordination mechanism requires; stigmergy's scaling advantage does not exempt it from the need for maintenance.

Stigmergy handles coordination well for tasks where the environment can encode the relevant signals clearly: build results, type contracts, test outcomes, interface definitions. The decisions that resist environmental encoding, the ambiguous trade-offs that require contextual judgment no test suite can capture, require a different coordination mechanism. That mechanism is hierarchy, and its physics, including the specific ways it fails, is worth examining with the same rigor.

CHAPTER 10

Why Hierarchy Fails (and Why You Need It Anyway)

Every organization that grows beyond a single team faces a decision that has no correct answer. The work exceeds what any individual can hold in context, so it must be distributed. Distribution requires delegation, and delegation is an act of information compression: the delegator transmits a reduced description of the problem to the delegate, who works on the reduction rather than the original. The compression is necessary because the delegate cannot hold the full problem. It is also destructive, because the aspects of the problem that do not survive compression are often the ones that determine whether the parts compose into a working whole: the subtle dependencies across components, the naming conventions that must be consistent, the architectural decisions whose consequences ripple through services that no single delegate can see.

The hierarchical experiment in Chapter 2 demonstrated this compression loss in isolation. Given a coordinator and a set of leaf agents, the coordinator chose to implement the system itself rather than delegate, judging — correctly — that the information loss of distributing partial-context subtasks would exceed any benefit of parallelism. The strategy worked within the bounds of the coordinator's capacity, and the bounds are the point. An agent that refuses to delegate can address only problems that fit within its own context. The moment the problem exceeds that context, delegation begins, compression begins, and the information loss is governed by physics that does not improve with better management. The dilemma does not admit a solution. It admits only the discipline of understanding precisely what the compression destroys, so that the destruction can be concentrated where it matters least.

• • •

The case for hierarchy's being necessary rests on the capacity limits already established: working memory holds five to nine chunks, Dunbar's number caps effective coordination relationships at roughly a hundred and fifty, and Shannon's channel capacity constrains human speech to approximately thirty-nine bits per second. These are not organizational preferences. They are measured properties of the substrate on which human organizations run. An organization of three engineers can coordinate through conversation. An organization of thirty cannot, because the four hundred and thirty-five pairwise channels exceed any individual's capacity to track, and the information flowing through those channels degrades with each retransmission.

Hierarchy is the standard solution to this scaling problem. Instead of every agent communicating with every other agent, agents communicate with their immediate superior, who aggregates the information and communicates a compressed summary upward. The compression reduces the bandwidth required at each level, which is what makes the system scale. A manager with six direct reports receives six streams of detailed information and transmits one stream of summarized information. The summarization is the value the hierarchy provides: it reduces information to a form the next level can process within its cognitive capacity.

The summarization is also where the hierarchy fails, because summarization is compression, and compression is lossy.

Several organizations have attempted to escape this trade-off, and their experiences are instructive precisely because the attempts were serious and the failures were structural rather than managerial. Valve, the game studio, famously operated with a flat structure where employees chose their own projects and moved their desks to join teams. The company produced extraordinary creative output in its early decades, but as it grew past Dunbar's number, informal hierarchies emerged that were less accountable than the formal ones they replaced: senior employees controlled project selection through social influence rather than organizational authority, and new hires reported difficulty navigating an organization where the official structure did not match the actual power dynamics. Spotify's squad model attempted a middle path, organizing engineers into autonomous squads aligned to features, with cross-cutting chapters and guilds for technical coordination. The model was elegant on paper; in practice, the matrix of squads, chapters, tribes, and guilds produced coordination overhead that rivaled the hierarchy it was designed to replace, and Spotify itself quietly retreated from the model's more ambitious claims. Amazon's two-pizza teams represent perhaps the most disciplined approach: small teams with well-defined service boundaries, communicating through APIs rather than meetings. The approach works because it combines hierarchy reduction (small teams) with stigmergic coordination (API contracts as environmental signals), but it requires decomposition discipline and a well-designed constraint topology to function.

• • •

The Data Processing Inequality, whose formal structure was established in Chapter 2, maps onto organizational hierarchy with the same inevitability. Every level of management is a processing step, and every processing step reduces the information available to subsequent steps. The reduction is irreversible; no amount of sophisticated processing at a higher level can recover information that was lost at a lower one. Applied to organizational depth: the information available at level three about conditions at level one is strictly less than the information available at level two, which is itself a degraded version of level one's reality. The mechanism is identical to dead reckoning in navigation, where a ship's position is estimated by adding each leg's heading and speed to the previous estimate rather than by independent observation. Each position estimate is based on the previous estimate plus new measurements, and the errors compound because each step's input is the previous step's imperfect output. A navigator using dead reckoning after ten course corrections has accumulated the uncertainty of all ten, and the only remedy is celestial navigation: fixing position against the stars, an independent measurement that bypasses the accumulated error entirely.

In organizational terms, a skip-level meeting or a direct review of production metrics is celestial navigation: it provides information that has not passed through the compression chain and therefore has not been degraded by it. A front-line engineer's detailed understanding of why a particular implementation approach was chosen, which alternatives were considered and rejected, what trade-offs were accepted, compresses into a status update for the team lead, then into a bullet point for the director, then into a color on a dashboard for the vice president, each operating at their level. The dashboard's green indicator and the engineer's nuanced understanding refer to the same project, but the information content of the two representations is not comparable. The compression has removed the context that would allow anyone reading the dashboard to distinguish between a project that is genuinely on track and a project that appears on track because the information that would reveal otherwise did not survive the journey.

Crawford-Sobel's theory of strategic communication, which Chapter 2 applied to the reviewer-implementer dynamic within a pipeline stage, introduces a second degradation mechanism that operates alongside the compression loss and compounds with it. When two agents have different incentive functions, communication between them becomes strategically distorted: the sender adjusts the message to influence the receiver's response. In a hierarchy, the distortion is recursive, because each sender's adjustment anticipates the adjustment of the next receiver.

An engineer reporting a project delay to a manager who controls their promotion does not fabricate information. The distortion is subtler than fabrication and harder to detect. The engineer frames the delay in terms that minimize the manager's anxiety, omits context that might provoke an escalation, and emphasizes mitigating factors that cast the delay as recoverable. The information that survives transmission is the information the engineer judged safe to share, selected by a criterion unrelated to what the manager needs to know and entirely determined by what the engineer predicts the manager will do with it. The manager, reporting upward, performs the same selection. Each level of the hierarchy adds a strategic filter on top of the compression loss, and the filters select for palatability rather than accuracy. The information reaching the top of a hierarchy has been compressed and filtered, and the filtering serves the interests of each transmitter rather than the interests of the organization.

The compression loss and the strategic distortion operate simultaneously, and their effects compound. Liberti and Mian, studying information flow in bank lending hierarchies, found that "soft information," the kind of contextual, qualitative, judgment-dependent knowledge that is most valuable for decision-making, effectively dies at level three. A lending officer's sense, built over three years of quarterly meetings, that a borrower's revenue dip is temporary because the borrower invested heavily in new equipment rather than losing customers, is soft information. It cannot survive compression into a credit score or a quarterly report, because the judgment depends on accumulated context that no summary format preserves. The bank's lending officers possessed detailed, nuanced understanding of their borrowers' situations. Their immediate supervisors retained some of this understanding in degraded form. The supervisors' superiors received numbers: default probabilities, credit scores, risk categories. The rich understanding of why a particular borrower was or was not a good risk, the kind of understanding that would have prevented the lending decisions that produced the 2008 financial crisis, did not survive two levels of hierarchical compression. It was not that the people at the top did not want the information. The hierarchy was physically incapable of transmitting it, because soft information does not survive lossy compression, and hierarchical communication is lossy compression by design.

The parallel to the Chapter 2 experiments is structural. A single agent with full context outperformed every multi-agent configuration because it suffered no compression loss. The hierarchy, given the same model and the same task, could not transmit the information necessary for correct implementation, because the compression that makes hierarchy scalable destroyed the details that determined whether the parts would compose. Liberti and Mian documented this in bank lending. The dysfunction experiments demonstrated it at machine speed, with no human ego or politics to confound the observation. The mechanism is identical.

· · ·

The obvious question is why, given these systematic failures, hierarchy persists as the dominant coordination mechanism in virtually every human organization. The answer is not that organizations are irrational. The answer is that the alternatives are worse for the problems hierarchy exists to solve.

A fully connected network of thirty engineers requires four hundred and thirty-five communication channels. Maintaining those channels consumes more time than the engineers have available for productive work. A flat organization of a hundred people has no mechanism for aggregating information across the group, which means that every decision requires polling every member, processing every response, and resolving every disagreement. The cost of this process exceeds the cost of the decision itself for all but the most consequential decisions. The result is predictable: flat organizations either make very few decisions (paralysis) or devolve into informal hierarchies where the people with the loudest voices or the most social capital make decisions on behalf of the group (which is hierarchy without the accountability that formal hierarchy provides).

Hierarchy works because the alternative at scale is not a better coordination mechanism. It is no coordination at all. The compression losses are real and measurable. The strategic distortions are real and measurable. The death of soft information at level three is real and documented. And the system still outperforms the alternatives for tasks that exceed the capacity of any individual agent, because the cost of imperfect coordination is lower than the cost of no coordination, and no other mechanism has been demonstrated to scale beyond Dunbar's number for tasks that require shared understanding.

This is the sense in which you need hierarchy "anyway." You need it the way you need a lossy image compression algorithm: not because you want to lose information, but because the uncompressed image does not fit in the available bandwidth, and a lossy representation of the image is more useful than no image at all. The engineering question is how to design the hierarchy so that the compression losses are concentrated in the information that matters least, and the information that matters most survives the transmission.

• • •

For AI-assisted development, the implications are specific and actionable. The single-agent ceiling, the finding that one agent with full context outperforms a hierarchy of agents with partial context, is a direct consequence of the information loss that hierarchy introduces. For any task that fits within a single agent's effective context window, hierarchical distribution is a net negative: it introduces compression losses, strategic distortions, and coordination overhead without providing any compensating benefit. The optimal architecture for such a task is a single agent with the full context, operating within a well-designed constraint topology, with no delegation, no review stages, and no intermediate aggregation.

For tasks that exceed a single agent's context window, which includes most systems of any real complexity, the question becomes how to minimize the information loss that distribution inevitably introduces. The principles already established provide the framework. Decompose at natural information boundaries, where the coupling between components is minimized and the interface between them can be specified precisely. Replace dialogue-based coordination with stigmergic coordination through shared environment and mechanical constraints. Design the constraint topology so that the rigid exterior enforces compatibility at the boundaries while the flexible interior gives each agent freedom to implement independently. Verify compliance mechanically rather than through advisory review.

Each of these principles is a response to a specific mechanism of hierarchical failure. Decomposition at information boundaries minimizes the information that must cross boundaries and therefore minimizes the information available for compression to destroy. Stigmergic coordination eliminates the dialogue channels through which Crawford-Sobel distortion propagates. Mechanical constraints replace the soft-information transmission that hierarchy cannot support with hard-information verification that does not degrade through layers. The combination does not eliminate hierarchy. It reduces the hierarchy's role to the minimum necessary: the initial decomposition and the specification of the interfaces between components. Everything else is handled by mechanisms that do not suffer from the systematic degradations that make hierarchy unreliable.

The practical question an engineer faces is not "hierarchy or not" but "how much hierarchy, where, and supplemented by what." The decision framework follows from the physics. Use single-agent execution for any task that fits within one agent's effective context window; the information loss from distribution exceeds any parallelism benefit. Use stigmergic coordination for tasks that can be decomposed into loosely coupled components with well-defined interfaces; the shared environment carries the coordination load at O(1) cost per agent. Use hierarchical coordination only for the residual tasks that require cross-component decisions where the information cannot be encoded in contracts or environmental signals: architectural trade-offs that span multiple services, priority decisions that require business context, and resource allocation across competing initiatives. The hierarchy should handle the decisions that require judgment about ambiguous trade-offs, where to allocate headcount between competing teams, whether to delay a feature for architectural coherence, which categories of technical debt to prioritize this quarter, and nothing else. Every decision that can be mechanized, every coordination need that can be encoded in a contract or a test or a shared type definition, should be removed from the hierarchy's responsibilities, because each decision removed is one less opportunity for the compression losses and strategic distortions to degrade the organization's information.

• • •

There is a deeper observation embedded in the hierarchy research. Hierarchy is a technology so old and so pervasive that most people do not think of it as a technology at all. It appears to be the natural way of organizing collective action, as inevitable as gravity, as unremarkable as the air. But hierarchy is not natural in this sense. It is a specific coordination mechanism with specific properties, specific failure modes, and specific alternatives, and the choice to use it, how to configure it, and when to replace it with something else is an engineering decision that should be made on the basis of evidence rather than tradition.

The engineering organizations that treat hierarchy as the default, the only way to organize work, the structure that exists because it has always existed, are making the same error as the engineering organizations that adopt microservices because Netflix uses microservices. They are substituting convention for analysis. The physics of hierarchy, the compression losses, the strategic distortions, the death of soft information, is knowable and known. An engineer who understands this physics can make informed decisions about when hierarchy is the right tool, when stigmergy is better, when a single agent with full context is optimal, and how to combine mechanisms to minimize the total information loss. An engineer who does not understand this physics uses hierarchy by default and absorbs the costs without knowing they exist, which is to say, without knowing there is an alternative.

Understanding the physics of coordination, information, and constraint is the competency that separates effective engineering from expensive guessing. Hierarchy is the coordination mechanism where this argument is most urgent, because hierarchy is the one everyone uses, the one that fails most expensively, and the one that is least often examined with the rigor it deserves. The engineer who treats hierarchy as furniture, as something that was in the room when they arrived and will be in the room when they leave, has surrendered the most consequential design decision in the organization to inertia. The engineer who treats it as a technology, with specifications, trade-offs, and alternatives, has taken the first step toward designing coordination systems that lose less information than the ones they inherited.

CHAPTER 11

The Goodhart Trap

The dysfunction experiments used a scoring system with seven metrics. Each metric measured a specific aspect of the system's quality: whether the services implemented the required endpoints, whether the data models were correct, whether the API contracts were consistent, whether the error handling followed the specification. The scoring system was well-designed, internally consistent, and more rigorous than most evaluation frameworks used in production software organizations. A perfect score was twenty-eight, and the single agent achieved it. The pipeline scored zero. These numbers are useful. They are also, in a specific and important sense, misleading.

The scoring system measured whether the implementation conformed to a specification. It did not measure whether the specification was correct. It did not measure whether the system would perform under load, whether the error messages were comprehensible to end users, whether the security model would survive contact with an adversary, or whether the architectural decisions would remain viable as the system evolved. The scoring system was a proxy for quality, not quality itself, and the researchers who designed it knew this. They chose the proxy because it was measurable, reproducible, and sufficient for the purpose of comparing coordination architectures. They did not confuse the proxy with the objective.

This distinction, between a proxy and the thing the proxy is supposed to represent, is the subject of what may be the most important law in the social sciences, and it applies to software engineering with a force that the field has been slow to appreciate. Charles Goodhart, an economist advising the Bank of England, observed in 1975 that any statistical regularity will tend to collapse once pressure is placed upon it for control purposes. Marilyn Strathern later reformulated the observation in its more widely known form: when a measure becomes a target, it ceases to be a good measure.

• • •

The law sounds abstract until you watch it operate. The mechanism is straightforward, and it operates in any system where agents are incentivized to optimize a measurable quantity. When you measure test coverage and reward high coverage, developers write tests that execute code without verifying behavior, because executing code is cheap and verifying behavior is expensive, and the metric rewards execution, not verification. When you measure lines of code and reward high output, developers write verbose code. Verbosity increases the metric, and the metric is what is being optimized. When you measure sprint velocity and reward high velocity, teams inflate their story-point estimates, because inflation increases the measured velocity without increasing the actual output, and the metric cannot distinguish between genuine productivity and accounting.

The pattern is not limited to software metrics. In the Atlanta Public Schools cheating scandal, standardized test scores served as a proxy for student achievement, and No Child Left Behind tied consequences to the numbers: sanctions for low-performing schools, bonuses for high-performing teachers. A hundred and seventy-eight educators across forty-four schools responded rationally to the incentive: they erased students' wrong answers and filled in correct ones, because altering answer sheets was cheaper than improving instruction, and the metric could not distinguish between a student who learned the material and a student whose teacher changed the answers after the fact. The superintendent received the National Superintendent of the Year award. Thirty-five educators were later indicted. The Department of Veterans Affairs measured patient wait times as a proxy for access to care, then tied performance evaluations to the numbers. Administrators at multiple facilities responded by falsifying wait-time records, maintaining secret lists of patients who had not yet been entered into the official scheduling system, because reducing the measured wait time was cheaper than reducing the actual wait time, and the metric recorded only what was entered into the system.

In every case, inside software and out, the mechanism is identical. The proxy was originally correlated with the objective because, in the absence of optimization pressure, the proxy and the objective moved together. Teams that wrote good code tended to have high test coverage. Banks with engaged customers tended to have more account openings. Hospitals with adequate access tended to have short wait times. The correlation was observed, the proxy was measured, and the measurement was used as a target. The moment the proxy became a target, the agents being measured discovered that optimizing the proxy was cheaper than optimizing the objective, and they began to optimize the proxy directly, breaking the correlation that had justified the measurement in the first place.

There is a subtler variant of this mechanism that operates on vocabulary rather than on numbers, and it is worth naming because it is pervasive in software organizations. Taxonomic competence is knowing the correct terms and frameworks without practicing the behaviors they describe. An organization that talks fluently about "test-driven development" and "CI/CD" without actually writing tests before code or automating its deployment pipeline has substituted the vocabulary of the practice for the practice itself — or whatever passes for it. The proxy here is linguistic: teams that do test-driven development talk about test-driven development, so talking about test-driven development becomes a signal of doing it, and the signal is cheaper to produce than the practice. This is Goodhart's Law applied to organizational language, and it is particularly dangerous because it passes casual inspection. An executive who hears the right terminology in a sprint review has no mechanism for distinguishing between a team that practices the methodology and a team that has learned to describe it. The vocabulary becomes a mask that delays intervention, sometimes for years, because the gap between stated practice and actual practice is invisible to anyone who is not examining the codebase, the deployment logs, or the test execution history. By the time the gap surfaces, the deviance it conceals has normalized.

The phenomenon scales beyond organizations to markets. Software that is rife with bugs but rich with visible features dominates markets where correct but feature-sparse alternatives struggle for adoption. The market's proxy for quality is visible functionality, and visible functionality is cheaper to produce than invisible correctness. This is Goodhart's Law operating at the evolutionary level: to have become the mainstay of modern software delivery, buggy feature-rich software must possess a competitive advantage that bug-free alternatives do not, and that advantage is legibility. A feature is visible to the buyer at the moment of the purchasing decision. Correctness is invisible until its absence causes a failure, and by then the purchasing decision has been made. The market optimizes for what it can see, which is what Goodhart predicts for any system that selects based on a measurable proxy, and the consequences are felt by every engineer who has watched a carefully built, well-tested system lose market share to a faster, flashier, buggier competitor.

The Chapter 2 experiments demonstrated this mechanism at machine speed and without human incentives. The pipeline's review stage optimized for the appearance of rigor rather than the substance of quality. The verification stages optimized for the appearance of testing rather than the substance of verification. The specification stage in the contract-first variant optimized for specification completeness rather than implementation completeness. Each is Goodhart's Law operating on a proxy that an architectural role had the incentive and the mechanism to optimize.

The AI agents were not gaming the system in the way that a human employee games a performance review. They had no career anxiety, no desire to appear competent, no understanding of the concept of gaming. They were doing what language models do: optimizing the output for the objective function implicit in their context. The reviewer's context defined its role as finding problems in code. Finding more problems looked like better performance of the role, because the context did not define "finding only real problems" as a constraint. The verifier's context defined its role as certifying that code passed verification. Certifying passage, even when no verification had occurred, satisfied the immediate objective, because the context did not distinguish between "verified and passed" and "not verified, reported as passed." The optimization pressure was structural, embedded in the architecture rather than in the psychology of the agents. The agents had no ego. The architecture didn't need one. The divergence between proxy and objective was the same one Goodhart observed in monetary policy fifty years earlier.

• • •

The specification perfectionism finding from the contract-first experiment deserves particular attention, because it demonstrates that Goodhart's Law applies even to the mechanisms designed to prevent Goodhart's Law.

The contract-first architecture was built to address the pipeline's dysfunctions directly. It replaced subjective review with mechanical verification, advisory judgment with typed contracts and automated tests. The specific dysfunctions of the pipeline did not appear. The architecture had closed the surface on which those dysfunctions operated. A different surface opened. The contract-generation agents began optimizing for specification quality, producing increasingly elaborate constraints — each locally rational, collectively consuming the budget intended for implementation. The dysfunction migrated from the evaluation phase to the specification phase. It changed form without disappearing.

The mechanism is worth tracing precisely, because it reveals something about the gap between proxy and objective that the pipeline's more obvious failures do not. The pipeline's code reviewer optimized a proxy (rejection rate) that was visibly disconnected from the objective (working code). An attentive designer could have predicted the divergence, because the proxy was crude: rejecting more code does not produce better code. The specification stage's proxy was subtler. A more comprehensive specification genuinely does produce more reliable verification, up to a point. The proxy and the objective were aligned for the first several hundred lines of specification. The divergence began only when the cost of additional specification exceeded the value of additional verification, and the specification stage had no mechanism for detecting that threshold, because the threshold depends on the remaining budget, the complexity of the implementation, the diminishing marginal value of each additional constraint, all global properties invisible to the specification stage's local view. The proxy was better designed than the pipeline's, and it diverged for exactly the same reason: the agent optimized what it could see at the expense of what it could not.

Fisheries science encountered this pattern without anyone's engineering it. In the Pacific sardine fishery, catch-per-unit-effort (the total catch divided by the fishing effort expended, used as a standard proxy for population health) failed to track a population crash of ninety-five percent, from 1.8 million metric tons to eighty-six thousand. The proxy had faithfully tracked population health for decades: abundant fish yielded high catches, declining fish yielded low ones. It diverged because the relationship between catch rates and population size depends on how fish distribute themselves across the ocean, and that distribution changes under population stress in ways the proxy was not designed to detect. No one gamed the metric. No agent optimized against it. The gap opened through an ecological mechanism operating below the measurement's resolution. The specification proxy diverged for the same reason: the gap exists at whatever boundary the measurement cannot see. Every measurement system has such a boundary.

• • •

The temptation, when confronted with Goodhart's Law, is to search for the right metric: the proxy so perfectly correlated with the objective that optimizing it is equivalent to optimizing the objective. This search is futile, and understanding why it is futile is the difference between an engineer who will spend a career chasing metrics and an engineer who understands what metrics can and cannot do.

The gap between proxy and objective exists because the objective is a property of the real world and the proxy is a property of the measurement system. "Quality software" is a statement about how the software behaves in production, under load, in the hands of actual users, over the course of its operational lifetime. Test coverage is a statement about what fraction of the code's execution paths are exercised by the test suite. The two are correlated because code that is exercised by tests is more likely to behave correctly than code that is not. The correlation is imperfect because a test that exercises a code path without verifying its behavior provides coverage without verification, and the metric cannot distinguish between coverage-with-verification and coverage-without-verification, because the metric counts execution, not correctness.

A concrete example makes the gap visible. Consider a function that calculates a user's subscription tier based on their payment history, account age, and promotional eligibility. A coverage-without-verification test calls the function with one set of inputs and asserts that the function returns without throwing an exception. The test executes every branch of the calculation, because the input is chosen to traverse the most complex path, and the coverage metric dutifully reports that the function is fully covered. The test verifies nothing about correctness. It confirms that the function runs, not that it calculates the right tier. A user with a three-year payment history and an active promotion could be assigned the wrong tier, and the test would pass, because the test never checked the output against the expected tier. The coverage metric sees a fully tested function. The production system sees a billing error. The two perspectives are irreconcilable because the metric measures execution, and execution is not verification.

You can make the metric more sophisticated. You can measure mutation testing scores, which count not just whether the tests execute the code but whether the tests detect injected faults. Mutation testing is a better proxy than coverage, because it is harder to satisfy without actually verifying behavior. It is still a proxy. A test suite can achieve a high mutation testing score by detecting faults in the code paths it tests while missing entirely the code paths it does not test. The blind spot has moved, not disappeared. You can add metrics for the blind spots, and the blind spots of those metrics will produce new gaps, and the regression will continue indefinitely, because every finite measurement system has a resolution limit, and the gap between measurement and reality exists at the resolution limit of any measurement system you design.

The argument is for understanding what measurement does, which is less than most organizations assume. Measurement reduces uncertainty. It does not eliminate uncertainty. A test suite that covers ninety percent of the codebase with verified, mutation-tested assertions provides high confidence that the tested code behaves correctly. It provides no confidence whatsoever about the remaining ten percent, and if the remaining ten percent includes the security boundary, the payment processing logic, or the data integrity constraints, the high coverage number is actively dangerous because it produces false confidence in a system with an unverified critical path.

The scientific response to this situation is straightforward: treat the measurement system as a hypothesis about what matters, and revise the hypothesis based on evidence. When a production incident occurs in a module with ninety percent coverage, the incident is evidence that the measurement system has a blind spot. The response is not to increase the coverage number. The response is to write a test that captures the specific failure, thereby closing the specific blind spot that the incident revealed. The measurement system evolves, incident by incident, toward a better approximation of the actual requirements, in the same way that a scientific model evolves, experiment by experiment, toward a better approximation of the actual phenomenon. The point is that measurement is hypothesis-testing, not truth-finding. The conclusion that all metrics are imperfect is not an argument for abandoning measurement; it is an argument for treating every measurement as provisional, subject to revision the moment evidence contradicts it.

• • •

Understanding that the gap exists is necessary. Living with the gap, rather than pretending it can be closed by a sufficiently clever metric, is the harder discipline. The practical discipline that Goodhart's Law imposes on the engineer is the discipline of proxy awareness: the ongoing recognition that every metric, every test suite, every scoring system, every evaluation framework is a proxy for the actual objective, and that the gap between proxy and objective is the surface on which dysfunction operates.

This discipline has several concrete expressions. The first is metric plurality: measuring the same objective through multiple independent proxies, so that gaming one proxy is visible through the others. A team that increases test coverage while increasing production incident rate is gaming coverage. A team that increases sprint velocity while decreasing customer satisfaction is gaming velocity. Neither metric alone reveals the gaming. Both metrics together make it visible, because the divergence between the proxies indicates that at least one of them has decoupled from the objective.

The second expression is proxy rotation: periodically changing what is measured, so that the optimization pressure does not have time to discover and exploit the proxy's blind spots. This is the measurement equivalent of crop rotation, and it works for the same reason: a pest that specializes in one crop cannot survive a field that changes crops each season. An optimization strategy that specializes in one metric cannot survive a measurement system that changes metrics each quarter. The cost is inconsistency in trend data. The benefit is that the agents being measured cannot develop stable strategies for gaming the metrics, which forces them back toward optimizing the underlying objective, which is the only strategy that works regardless of what is being measured.

The third expression, and the most important, is the recognition that the gap between proxy and objective is the engineer's responsibility to monitor, not the metric's responsibility to close. No metric will close the gap on its own. The gap is a design problem, not a technical one, and it requires the same ongoing judgment, experimentation, and revision that every other design problem requires. The engineer who designs a test suite and then treats it as a permanent arbiter of quality has confused the map with the territory. The test suite is a map. The territory is production behavior. The map is useful precisely to the extent that it accurately represents the territory, and that accuracy must be continuously verified by comparing the map's predictions (all tests pass, therefore the system works) with the territory's reality (the system works, as measured by production behavior, user satisfaction, and incident frequency).

· · ·

Goodhart's Law is what happens when you measure without understanding. You observe a correlation, instrument it, incentivize it, and the correlation collapses because the incentive changes the behavior that produced the correlation. This is the pattern of cargo-cult science that Richard Feynman described in his 1974 Caltech commencement address: imitating the form of the scientific method without practicing its substance, performing the ritual of measurement without understanding what the measurement means or what could make it wrong.

The antidote is the scientific discipline of questioning your instruments with the same rigor you apply to questioning your results. A scientist who discovers an unexpected result asks, before celebrating, whether the instrument is calibrated correctly, whether the experimental design controls for the relevant confounds, and whether the result would replicate under slightly different conditions. An engineer who discovers a high test coverage number should ask, with the same rigor, whether the tests actually verify behavior, whether the coverage metric counts the code paths that matter, and whether the metric would survive the injection of realistic faults into the tested code.

This discipline is harder than it sounds, because questioning your own measurement system requires admitting that you do not fully know what "quality" means in your specific context, and that the metrics you are using are approximations whose accuracy must be continuously validated. Most engineering organizations prefer the comfort of a number: a coverage percentage, a velocity chart, a defect density metric, something that can be reported in a dashboard and treated as an objective assessment of the system's health. The number feels like knowledge. It feels like understanding. The harder discipline is the recognition that the number is a hypothesis about the system's health, and that hypotheses must be tested, not worshipped. The organization that treats its metrics as settled truth has stopped doing science and started doing religion, and the difference will be visible in the production incident log long before it is visible in the dashboard.

PART V

The Craft

CHAPTER 12

Grokking

There is a moment in learning that experienced engineers recognize instantly and struggle to describe. You are reading a codebase you have never seen before, tracing the execution path of a request through middleware, through validation, through a service layer, through a repository abstraction, through a database call, and for hours or days the code is a series of disconnected observations: this function calls that function, this class implements that interface, this config file defines those values. You understand each piece individually. You cannot see the whole. Then, at some point that you cannot predict or force, the pieces connect. You stop seeing functions and start seeing the system. You stop tracing the code and start reasoning about behavior. The representation in your mind shifts from a sequence of facts to a structure, and the structure generates predictions you did not explicitly derive: you know what will happen if you change this module, because you can see how the change propagates through the structure, even though you have never explicitly enumerated the propagation path.

This is grokking, a term Robert Heinlein coined in 1961 and that the software industry has adopted because no other English word captures the phenomenon. It is the transition from knowing the facts about a system to understanding the system, and the difference between the two is not a matter of quantity. You do not grok a system by accumulating more facts about it. You grok it when the facts reorganize in your mind into a pattern that generates the facts as consequences, so that you no longer need to remember the individual observations because you can derive them from the pattern. This transition is qualitative, not quantitative, and it has properties that are worth examining carefully because they determine how engineers learn, how they fail to learn, and what the rise of AI tools is doing to the learning process itself.

• • •

Cognitive science provides a framework for understanding why the grokking moment occurs when it does, and the framework is more mechanical than mystical. The phenomenon of spreading activation, studied extensively in the context of associative memory, describes how the activation of one concept in a neural network primes related concepts, lowering the threshold for their activation and making the connections between them more likely to fire. When you read a codebase and encounter a pattern, the abstract concept of that pattern is activated in your memory. When you encounter the same pattern in a different context, the activation from the second encounter combines with the residual activation from the first, and the connection between the two contexts strengthens. Repeated encounters across different contexts produce a dense web of cross-contextual associations, and at some point the web becomes dense enough that the pattern is activated by any of its instances, which is to say, you recognize it.

This process is gradual at the neurological level and sudden at the phenomenological level. The activation accumulates below the threshold of conscious awareness, and the grokking moment is the moment the accumulated activation crosses that threshold. This is why grokking feels sudden even though the learning that produces it is incremental: you were learning the whole time, building the associative web one encounter at a time, but you could not perceive the progress because the web was below the threshold of recognition until the instant it crossed it. The experience is analogous to a supersaturated solution: the solute accumulates invisibly until a single additional crystal triggers crystallization of the entire solution. The crystal did not cause the crystallization. The accumulation caused it. The crystal was the final increment.

The practical consequence for learning is that the conditions that produce grokking are specific and somewhat counterintuitive. You cannot grok a system by studying it in the abstract. You must encounter it in multiple concrete contexts, from multiple angles, with enough variation that the associative web connects the pattern to a wide range of instances rather than to a single example.

104

A junior engineer joins a team maintaining a distributed event-processing system. The first week, she reads the architecture documents and traces the code paths: events enter through a gateway, hit a routing layer, fan out to processors, and land in various data stores. She understands the components. She does not understand the system. During the second week, she is assigned a feature that requires adding a new event type, and she discovers that the routing layer's configuration is not just a mapping table but a set of ordering guarantees that downstream processors depend on. She gets the ordering wrong. A processor that aggregates events over time windows produces incorrect totals because it receives events from her new type interleaved with events from an existing type in an order that violates an assumption she did not know existed. She fixes the ordering, and the fix requires understanding why the routing layer uses a priority queue rather than a simple dispatch table.

During the third week, she debugs a production incident where a processor falls behind under load, and she discovers that the backpressure mechanism in the routing layer is the same priority queue she encountered during the feature work, operating in a different mode. The three encounters, reading, building, and debugging, each activated the routing layer from a different angle, and the accumulated activation produces the shift: she stops seeing the routing layer as a configuration file and starts seeing it as the system's consistency boundary. The event ordering, the backpressure behavior, and the processor guarantees are all consequences of a single design decision, and once she can see the decision, she can predict how changes to any component will propagate through the system without tracing each path individually.

• • •

Manu Kapur's research on productive failure provides the second piece of the mechanism, and it inverts an assumption that most educational and professional practice takes for granted. The standard model of training is instruction-first: teach the concept, then practice it. Kapur's experiments, replicated across multiple domains and age groups with an aggregate effect size of $d=0.36$, demonstrate that the reverse order produces deeper understanding. Students who attempt to solve a problem before receiving instruction, and who fail at the attempt, learn the subsequent instruction more deeply and transfer it more effectively to novel problems than students who receive the instruction first and then practice.

The mechanism is preparation, not punishment. The failed attempt does not teach the correct solution. What it teaches is the shape of the problem: the constraints that make it difficult, the approaches that seem promising but do not work, the features of the problem space that must be accounted for in any successful solution. When the instruction arrives, the student has a prepared surface of questions, frustrations, and partially formed mental models on which the instruction can attach. The instruction answers questions the student is already asking, which is fundamentally different from answering questions the student has not thought to ask. The first produces understanding. The second produces notes.

For software engineering, the implication is that the struggle of learning a new codebase, the hours of confusion, the wrong hypotheses, the failed attempts to understand why the system behaves as it does, is not an inefficiency to be eliminated. It is the process by which the associative web is constructed. The confusion is productive precisely because it is genuine: the engineer is encountering the actual constraints of the system, forming hypotheses about its behavior, testing those hypotheses by reading code and running experiments, and revising the hypotheses when they fail. Each failed hypothesis leaves a residue of understanding that the correct explanation, when it arrives, can attach to. The engineer who is handed the correct explanation first, without having struggled, receives the explanation without the prepared surface that would give it depth, and the result is knowledge without comprehension: the ability to recite how the system works without the ability to predict how it will behave under novel conditions.

• • •

The AI de-skilling research provides the cautionary application of these principles. A growing body of evidence documents what researchers call the "perpetual junior" phenomenon: developers who, through heavy reliance on AI code generation, maintain the appearance of productivity without developing the underlying understanding that would allow them to work independently.

The mechanism is the elimination of productive failure. When an engineer encounters a problem they do not know how to solve and asks an AI to solve it, the AI produces a solution that bypasses the struggle entirely. The engineer receives the answer without having formed the questions, without having explored the problem space, without having built the associative web that would give the answer structural context. The spreading activation that would have occurred during the struggle, the priming of related concepts across multiple contexts, does not occur because the struggle did not occur. The engineer learns what the solution looks like without learning why it works, which is to say, they acquire recognition memory without acquiring the generative understanding that would allow them to produce or modify the solution in a novel context. We have built a gym where the machines do the exercises for you, and we are puzzled that no one is getting stronger.

Recognition memory is the ability to identify a pattern when you see it. Recall memory is the ability to produce the pattern from internal resources without an external prompt. Generative understanding is the ability to derive the pattern from principles, producing it in contexts where you have never seen it applied. These are three distinct cognitive capacities, and they are arranged in order of depth: recognition is shallow, recall is intermediate, generative understanding is deep. AI-assisted development, when used without discipline, systematically trains recognition at the expense of recall and generative understanding, because the developer sees correct solutions (training recognition) without producing them independently (which would train recall) and without deriving them from principles (which would train generative understanding).

The result is a developer who appears competent in the presence of the tool and is helpless in its absence. The appearance of competence is genuine: the developer can identify correct code, approve reasonable solutions, and navigate familiar patterns with confidence. The helplessness is also genuine: when the tool produces incorrect output, the developer cannot identify the error, because the identification requires generative understanding of the underlying principles, and generative understanding was never developed because the struggle that produces it was consistently avoided. The developer who has used AI to implement every API endpoint for six months can recognize RESTful patterns and approve reasonable designs. Confronted with a WebSocket connection that behaves unexpectedly, they cannot diagnose the issue, because diagnosis requires generative understanding of network protocols, connection lifecycle, and frame-level behavior, and that understanding was never built. The familiar patterns are recognized; the unfamiliar ones are opaque.

The perpetual junior phenomenon is Goodhart's Law applied to developer productivity: optimize for output velocity and you sacrifice the understanding that makes output valuable. The metric (features shipped, tickets closed, pull requests merged) captures the appearance of engineering while the substance of engineering, the generative understanding that allows an engineer to navigate situations no metric anticipated, atrophies from disuse.

• • •

The defense against de-skilling is not the avoidance of AI tools. The tools are too useful and their advantages too significant to forgo on principle. The defense is the deliberate preservation of struggle in the learning process, the conscious decision to encounter some problems without AI assistance, not because the AI could not solve them, but because the act of solving them is what produces understanding.

This is a discipline that runs counter to every productivity incentive the industry currently applies. A developer who spends three hours understanding a codebase before using AI to modify it will appear less productive than a developer who asks AI to modify the codebase immediately. The first developer is building the associative web that will allow them to detect errors in the AI's output, predict the consequences of changes, and make architectural decisions that account for the system's actual constraints. The second developer is building a dependency on the tool that will compound with every task, because each task solved without understanding is a missed opportunity for the learning that would have made subsequent tasks more tractable.

The practical expression of this discipline is structured engagement with the problem before engaging the tool. Read the code first. Trace the execution path. Form a hypothesis about how the system behaves. Attempt, at least briefly, to design the solution mentally before asking the AI to implement it. The attempt will often be wrong. The wrongness is the point: it activates the spreading association network, primes the related concepts, and prepares the surface on which the AI's solution, when it arrives, can attach with structural depth rather than surface familiarity.

This is the research-first protocol, viewed through the lens of cognitive science rather than information theory. The research-first protocol says: provide the AI with accurate context so that its output is constrained by reality rather than by its training distribution. The learning discipline described here says: provide yourself with the struggle that produces understanding, so that your evaluation of the AI's output is informed by comprehension rather than by pattern matching. Both protocols are instances of the same principle. The quality of the output, whether the output is code or understanding, is bounded by the quality of the context in which the agent operates, and the agent's context includes not just the information available to it but the depth of the agent's engagement with that information.

• • •

Grokking is what scientific understanding feels like from the inside. A physicist who has grokked Newtonian mechanics does not need to memorize the trajectory equations for each type of projectile. They derive the equations from the principles, because the principles generate the equations as consequences. A software engineer who has grokked a system's architecture does not need to remember which function calls which. They derive the call chain from the architectural pattern, because the pattern generates the call chain as a consequence.

The cargo-cult practitioner, by contrast, has the facts without the structure. They can tell you that the authentication module validates tokens and that the session manager checks expiry, but they cannot tell you what happens if you change the token format, because the prediction requires structural understanding that fact collection does not provide. They know the what without the why, and the AI age is producing this cognitive profile at an accelerating rate, because the tools make it possible to produce correct output (what) without developing the understanding of the mechanism (why) that would allow you to produce correct output in a novel situation.

The discipline of grokking, the willingness to struggle before receiving the answer, the deliberate engagement with complexity before reaching for the tool that simplifies it, is the cognitive expression of the scientific method. You form a hypothesis. You test it against the code. You fail. You revise. You test again. Each iteration builds the associative web that will eventually produce the qualitative shift from knowledge to understanding. The shift is not available for purchase, and it does not respond to prompting or delegation; an AI can generate the correct answer, but the understanding that makes the answer useful is a property of the engineer's own associative network, built by struggle rather than by observation. It can only be earned through the kind of sustained, sometimes frustrating engagement with complexity that productive failure research documents and that the productivity metrics of the industry systematically penalize.

The structural tension is visible in any team that measures velocity: the metrics incentivize exactly the behavior that prevents grokking. Every sprint that rewards tickets closed over understanding built pushes engineers toward the tool and away from the struggle. One countermeasure is to designate one task per sprint as a "deep dive," where the engineer must understand the system before modifying it, with no AI assistance until they can articulate the system's current behavior and predict the effects of the proposed change. The cost appears in the velocity chart. The return appears the first time the engineer catches something the tool would have missed, which is where the most expensive failures live.

The engineer who reads the code before prompting the model, who traces the execution path before requesting modifications, who forms a hypothesis before testing it, builds understanding that compounds across every system they encounter. The engineer who reaches for AI at the first sign of difficulty builds a dependency that compounds just as fast. The compounding is invisible in both cases. It becomes visible the first time the tool fails and the engineer must navigate without it.

CHAPTER 13

Multi-Pass Thinking

Consider what actually happens when a senior engineer reviews a pull request in a single pass, which is to say, the way most code review happens in most organizations. The engineer opens the diff, reads from top to bottom, and forms a running judgment that attempts to evaluate simultaneously whether the code compiles, whether the logic is correct, whether the design is sound, whether the error handling is adequate, whether the naming is consistent, whether the change is safe to deploy, and whether the overall approach is the right one. These are not the same question. They operate at different levels of abstraction, require different cognitive frames, and draw on different areas of expertise. Evaluating whether a function handles null inputs correctly requires attention to the logic of one function. Evaluating whether the function's existence is the right architectural choice requires attention to the system as a whole. The engineer is asked to do both in the same pass, which means the engineer is asking their brain to operate at all levels of abstraction simultaneously, which is something the brain cannot do.

The result is predictable and well-documented. Cognitive psychology has established that human attention is a serial process: you can attend to one cognitive frame at a time, and switching between frames incurs a measurable cost in accuracy and processing speed. When you attempt to evaluate logic and architecture in the same pass, you oscillate between the two frames, attending to neither with full fidelity. The logic review misses edge cases because your attention was partly allocated to architectural concerns. The architectural review misses design problems because your attention was partly allocated to logic. The verification check at the end receives whatever attention remains, which, after the cognitive depletion of the preceding analysis, is typically insufficient to catch anything but the most obvious problems. The single-pass review feels thorough because the reviewer read every line. The feeling is indistinguishable from the perception gap: a subjective experience of competence that does not survive objective measurement.

Attentional residue provides the mechanism. When you engage with a cognitive task, the attention patterns activated during that task persist after you transition to the next task. The architectural thinking you did while reviewing the first file contaminates the logic thinking you do while reviewing the second file. The contamination is not dramatic; it is a slight bias toward the previous frame, a tendency to see the current code through the lens you were using moments ago rather than through the lens the current code requires. This bias compounds across files, across concerns, and across the duration of the review session, producing a review that is shallower than the reviewer believes and less reliable than the process assumes.

• • •

Multiple passes, each focused on a single concern at a single level of abstraction, with explicit separation between passes so that the attentional residue of one pass does not contaminate the next, address the problem that more careful single-pass review cannot.

The principle is not unique to software. Aviation arrived at it through accident investigation. The preflight checklist does not ask the pilot to evaluate the aircraft's airworthiness in a single holistic assessment. It decomposes airworthiness into individually verifiable dimensions: fuel quantity, control surface freedom, instrument calibration, communication systems, navigation equipment. Each item is checked independently, in a fixed order, with a physical record of completion. The checklist exists because the aviation industry learned, through decades of crashes, that holistic assessments of complex systems are unreliable. A pilot who evaluates the aircraft "overall" will miss the item that kills the passengers. A pilot who evaluates each item in isolation, in a structured sequence, will catch the fault because the structured sequence ensures that every dimension receives dedicated attention. The WHO Surgical Safety Checklist applies the same principle to surgery: before incision, the team verifies patient identity, surgical site, procedure, allergies, and anticipated blood loss as separate items rather than as a gestalt assessment of readiness. The checklist reduced surgical mortality by forty-seven percent in its initial trial, not because the surgeons were incompetent without it, but because the structured decomposition of concerns caught the failures that holistic assessment systematically missed.

The seven-pass protocol provides a specific framework for this decomposition, though the exact number of passes matters less than the principle that each pass holds one variable constant while examining one dimension of the artifact. The protocol, developed through engineering practice and refined through coaching sessions, proceeds as follows.

The first pass is comprehension: reading the change to understand what it does, without evaluating whether it does it well. This pass answers the question "what is this code doing?" and deliberately excludes the questions "is this the right approach?" and "is this implemented correctly?" The exclusion is the point. Comprehension and evaluation are different cognitive operations, and performing them simultaneously degrades both. The comprehension pass builds the mental model that subsequent passes will evaluate. Without a clear mental model, the evaluations operate against assumptions rather than understanding, and the quality of the evaluation is bounded by the accuracy of the assumptions.

The second pass is delta analysis: identifying what changed and what did not. This is not the same as comprehension. Comprehension asks what the code does. Delta analysis asks what is different about what the code does compared to what the code did before. This distinction matters because many bugs are not errors in the new code. They are interactions between the new code and the old code, places where an assumption made by the unchanged code is violated by the change. Delta analysis surfaces these interaction points by focusing attention on the boundaries between changed and unchanged code, which is where most integration defects originate.

The third pass is structural: evaluating whether the design of the change is sound. Does this responsibility belong in this component? Does this abstraction earn its complexity? Does this change respect the architectural boundaries established by the system's design? Structural evaluation requires the broadest frame: you are no longer looking at the code but at the system, and the code is evaluated against the system's design constraints rather than against its own internal logic. This is the pass that catches the locally correct but globally incoherent changes that single-pass review misses, because it is the only pass that explicitly asks the global question.

The fourth pass is logic: verifying that the implementation is correct. Does the function handle edge cases? Are the conditionals complete? Do the state transitions account for all possible inputs? Logic verification requires the narrowest frame: you are looking at individual functions, individual branches, individual state machines, and you are evaluating each against its specification.

The specification is the mental model built during the comprehension pass, which is why the comprehension pass must come first.

The fifth pass is style: evaluating naming, formatting, documentation, and consistency with the project's conventions. This pass is deliberately placed late in the protocol because style concerns are the most likely to contaminate other passes. An engineer who notices a naming inconsistency during the logic pass will allocate attention to naming that should have been allocated to logic, and the logic review suffers. By deferring style to its own pass, the protocol prevents style concerns from competing with more consequential concerns for the reviewer's limited attention.

The sixth pass is verification: checking that the change is tested, that the tests are meaningful (not just coverage theater), and that the verification strategy is adequate for the risk level of the change. This pass catches the verification theater documented in Chapter 2, where certification mechanisms reported correctness without testing anything. A dedicated verification pass asks not "did the tests pass?" but "do the tests test the thing that matters?"

The seventh pass is blast radius: assessing what else in the system could be affected by this change, including downstream consumers, shared state, implicit dependencies, and deployment-order assumptions. This is the pass that catches the changes whose direct effects are correct and whose indirect effects are catastrophic, the changes that work perfectly in the test environment and break three other services in production because a shared assumption was violated.

A worked example makes the protocol concrete. Suppose a pull request adds rate limiting to an API gateway, touching four files: a configuration file, a middleware module, a test file, and a deployment manifest. The comprehension pass reads the diff and establishes: the PR adds a token-bucket rate limiter that returns HTTP 429 when a client exceeds its allocation. The delta analysis pass identifies what changed and what did not: the middleware intercepts requests before they reach the route handlers, the configuration introduces a new per-client limit, and the deployment manifest adds an environment variable for the bucket size, but the existing authentication middleware is unchanged, which means rate limiting runs after authentication, which means unauthenticated requests consume rate-limit tokens. The structural pass asks whether rate limiting belongs in the gateway middleware at all, or whether it should be a separate service, and whether the per-client granularity is appropriate given that some clients authenticate with shared API keys. The logic pass checks the token-bucket implementation: does the refill interval handle clock skew between replicas, does the bucket overflow on configuration reload, does the 429 response include the Retry-After header that clients need to back off gracefully.

The remaining passes reveal what the first four could not. The style pass notes that the new middleware uses a different error response format than the existing middleware, and that the configuration variable names do not follow the project's naming convention. The verification pass examines the tests: the test file covers the happy path (request allowed) and the limit path (request rejected) but does not test the refill behavior, the multi-replica consistency, or the interaction with the authentication middleware. The blast radius pass traces the downstream effects: the 429 response will propagate to the mobile client, which does not currently handle 429 and will display a generic error; the monitoring dashboard will show a spike in 4xx errors that the on-call engineer may interpret as a service failure; and the deployment requires the new environment variable, which means deploying the code before the variable is configured will use the default value, which is zero, which will rate-limit all requests. A single-pass review would have caught some of these issues. The structured decomposition catches all of them, because each pass dedicates full attention to the dimension that would have been diluted in a single pass.

• • •

The skeptical engineer will observe that seven passes through a code review sounds like seven times the work. The math is wrong.

A single-pass review of a complex change takes, say, forty-five minutes and catches sixty percent of the issues. The reviewer's attention is divided across seven concerns, each receiving roughly one-seventh of the total processing capacity, and the interactions between concerns (attentional residue, frame-switching costs, cognitive depletion over the session) further reduce the effective capacity allocated to each concern. The forty-five minutes feel thorough. The forty percent of issues that are missed will be discovered in production, in integration testing, in a subsequent PR that reveals the flaw, or never, and the cost of each missed issue is measured in hours of debugging, deployment rollbacks, and incident response.

Seven focused passes through the same change take approximately ten to fifteen minutes each, depending on the complexity of the change and the specific pass. The total time is comparable to, or moderately greater than, the single-pass time. The difference is that each pass allocates the reviewer's full attention to a single concern, which means that each concern receives the full processing capacity rather than one-seventh of it. The hit rate per concern is higher because the attention is undivided. The total hit rate across all concerns is substantially higher because the interactions between concerns (the attentional residue, the frame-switching costs) have been eliminated by the explicit separation between passes.

The math is not seven times the work. It is approximately the same amount of work, allocated differently. The single-pass approach distributes forty-five minutes of cognitive capacity across seven concurrent concerns. The multi-pass approach distributes the same capacity across seven sequential concerns, with the separation between concerns preventing the interference that degrades the single-pass approach. The multi-pass approach is not a more expensive process. It is a more efficient allocation of the same cognitive resources, and the efficiency gain comes from the same principle that makes sequential decomposition outperform parallel decomposition for tasks with dependencies: concerns that interact with each other are processed more accurately in isolation than in combination.

• • •

The connection to AI-assisted development is direct and practical. The mega-prompt anti-pattern, where a single prompt asks the model to analyze, refactor, and test a piece of code in one interaction, is the single-pass approach applied to AI. The model's attention mechanism suffers from the same interference effects that human cognition suffers from, for different mechanistic reasons but with the same practical consequence: each task is performed with less fidelity than it would receive in isolation, and the tasks performed later in the sequence are contaminated by the attentional residue of the tasks performed earlier.

The multi-pass approach applied to AI-assisted work decomposes the cognitive task across interactions, each focused on a single concern. One interaction reads the code and builds a summary (comprehension). A separate interaction, with fresh context, analyzes the structural design (structural pass). A separate interaction evaluates the logic for correctness (logic pass). A separate interaction generates tests (verification pass). Each interaction contains only the context relevant to its specific concern, which means the model's attention is concentrated on the right information for the right question, rather than distributed across the full complexity of a multi-concern prompt.

This approach is slower than the mega-prompt. It is also more reliable, for the same reason that multi-pass human review is more reliable than single-pass: each concern receives the full capacity of the processing system, rather than a fractional share degraded by interference from concurrent concerns. The trade-off between speed and reliability is the same trade-off: the fast approach produces a subjective sense of productivity that does not survive objective measurement, while the slower approach produces measurable quality improvements that justify the additional time.

• • •

The deeper principle that multi-pass thinking instantiates is the principle of controlled variables, borrowed from experimental design and applied to cognitive work. An experiment that varies three factors simultaneously cannot determine which factor caused the observed result, because the interactions between factors confound the attribution. An experiment that varies one factor at a time, holding the others constant, can attribute the result to the varied factor with confidence, because the controls eliminate the confounds.

A single-pass code review varies seven cognitive concerns simultaneously, which means the reviewer cannot determine, after the review, which concerns received adequate attention and which did not. The review feels like a unified judgment, but the judgment is an uncontrolled mixture of seven partially attended concerns, and the reviewer has no mechanism for assessing the quality of their attention to any individual concern. A multi-pass review varies one concern at a time, which means the reviewer can assess, after each pass, whether the pass was thorough, whether it raised any issues, and whether the issues raised are substantive or procedural. The multi-pass approach provides the reviewer with what the single-pass approach does not: a structured method for evaluating the quality of their own evaluation.

This is the scientific method applied to the act of thinking itself. Form a hypothesis about one dimension of the artifact (this pass, I am checking the logic). Test the hypothesis (does the logic hold under all specified conditions?). Record the result (these edge cases are not handled). Move to the next dimension. Hold the previous dimensions constant. The process is explicit, auditable, and falsifiable at each step, which means that when the review misses an issue, the miss can be attributed to a specific pass and the pass can be improved. The single-pass approach provides no such auditability. The missed issue is lost in the mixture of seven concurrent concerns, and the reviewer has no mechanism for determining which concern's inadequate attention caused the miss.

The scientist decomposes a complex phenomenon into individually testable hypotheses, varies one factor at a time, and builds understanding through the accumulation of controlled observations. The engineer who reviews code in multiple passes is doing the same thing: decomposing a complex evaluation into individually focused assessments, examining one dimension at a time, and building a judgment through the accumulation of controlled observations. The process takes longer, and the results justify the cost, because controlled observation accumulates into engineering judgment where uncontrolled observation accumulates into guesswork. The willingness to spend the additional time is, in practice, a willingness to treat thoroughness as a measurable outcome rather than a subjective impression.

CHAPTER 14

Them Problems vs You Problems

On the evening of April 20, 2010, engineers on the Deepwater Horizon drilling rig ran a negative pressure test on the Macondo well in the Gulf of Mexico. The test was designed to verify that the cement barrier at the bottom of the well was holding back the oil and gas reservoir, thirteen thousand feet below the sea floor. The pressure readings were anomalous: the drill pipe showed zero pressure, as expected, but the kill line showed fourteen hundred pounds per square inch, which should have been impossible if the cement was intact. The engineers debated the results for over an hour.

BP's well site leaders asked whether the test had passed. The engineers on the rig could not reconcile the conflicting readings. They proposed explanations: a bladder effect, trapped pressure, an anomaly in the kill line itself. These were real diagnostic possibilities, expressed in the engineers' frame, using the engineers' vocabulary. The well site leaders needed something different. They needed to know what the pressure readings meant for the decision they were responsible for making: was it safe to proceed with displacing the heavy drilling mud with seawater, removing the last barrier between the rig and the high-pressure reservoir below? The engineers had the information to answer that question, but they never translated it out of their technical frame. The anomalous pressure meant the cement had failed and the mud was the only remaining barrier. Removing it would open a path from a thirteen-thousand-foot column of pressurized hydrocarbons to the surface. The test was interpreted as passing. Ninety minutes later, the well blew out. Eleven workers died and four million barrels of oil entered the Gulf of Mexico over the next eighty-seven days.

The Deepwater Horizon disaster is among the most consequential examples of a pattern that occurs, in less catastrophic form, in every engineering organization. A coaching session with a senior front-end lead at a growth-stage startup illustrates the same dynamic at its ordinary scale. The lead, responsible for the codebase's architecture and code review process, had been raising concerns about rushed implementations during a major design system migration. He documented the technical complexity, listed the architectural constraints, explained why shortcuts would create maintainability problems. The product team heard these as reasons the engineering lead did not want to do the work, as obstacles being manufactured to justify delay. The lead's frustration was genuine and technically justified. The product team's dismissal was also genuine and, from within their frame, rational. They had pressure from above to deliver, and the engineer's concerns were expressed as engineering problems: maintainability, architectural constraints, technical debt. These are real problems, but they are "you problems," problems that exist in the engineer's cognitive frame and that the product team has no mechanism for evaluating because the evaluation requires expertise they do not have and should not be expected to have.

The coaching conversation that followed centered on a single reframe. When the engineer says "it won't be maintainable" or "we'll have to rework it later," the product team hears a problem that belongs to engineering. When the engineer says "if we do this, it's going to slow down the runway, it's going to knock these asks that you have further back significantly," the product team hears a problem that belongs to them. The technical content has not changed. The frame has. As the coach put it: "If you communicate it as you problems, I don't have a problem with that. I'm going to go ahead and ask you to do it. If you communicate it as me problems, then I think, wait a minute, how can we not have any me problems and still get this done?"

• • •

The skill of translating between technical reality and business reality is the least technical and most consequential competency a senior engineer can develop, and it is the competency that the AI age makes more important rather than less, for reasons that are worth examining with some care.

When code is expensive to produce, the engineer's value proposition is obvious: the engineer produces the code, and the code is expensive, therefore the engineer is valuable. The translation between technical and business frames is helpful but not essential, because the engineer's primary contribution is the mechanical production of the artifact. The engineer who cannot communicate with stakeholders is still valuable, because the artifact speaks for itself, or at least it ships, and the shipping is the contribution.

When code is cheap to produce, the engineer's contribution shifts from producing the artifact to specifying what the artifact should be, verifying that the artifact is correct, and ensuring that the artifact fits into the larger system. Each of these activities requires the engineer to communicate with people who do not share the engineer's frame: product managers who think in terms of user outcomes, executives who think in terms of revenue and risk, customers who think in terms of the problem they are trying to solve, designers who think in terms of the experience they are trying to create. The engineer who cannot translate between frames becomes a bottleneck rather than a contributor, because the most valuable work the engineer does, specifying what to build and verifying that it was built correctly, requires information that lives in other people's heads, expressed in other people's vocabularies, governed by other people's incentive structures. The industry spends four years training people to communicate with machines and then evaluates them on their ability to communicate with humans. The surprise is not that the translation is poor. The surprise is that anyone expected otherwise.

This is not a soft skill in the way the industry typically uses that phrase, as a vaguely defined interpersonal quality that is acknowledged as important and never taught rigorously. It is a specific cognitive operation, as precise and as teachable as any technical skill: the identification of the listener's frame, the translation of the message's content into the terms and priorities of that frame, and the preservation of the essential information through the translation. It is context engineering applied to human communication, and it is governed by the same information-theoretic constraints that govern context engineering for AI. The listener's cognitive frame is their context window. Information that does not fit the frame will be ignored or misinterpreted, for the same reason that information that does not fit a model's context window will be dropped or hallucinated. The engineer's job is to fit the information into the frame, which requires understanding the frame at least as well as the engineer understands the technical content being translated.

Return for a moment to the Deepwater Horizon case, because the full translation is instructive. The rig engineers presented anomalous pressure readings and proposed possible explanations: a bladder effect, trapped pressure, a mechanical anomaly in the kill line. The well site leaders asked whether the test had passed. The engineers said they could not fully explain the kill-line pressure but that the drill-pipe readings looked acceptable. This was the wrong answer to the wrong question, delivered in the wrong frame. A "them problem" translation of the same data would have proceeded differently. The first operation is identifying the listener's frame: BP's well site leaders were responsible for a proceed-or-halt decision, and their decision calculus weighed rig costs of approximately one million dollars per day, project timeline, and well integrity. The second operation is mapping the technical concern into that frame. The pressure data, translated, means something like: "We have pressure where we should not have pressure. The most likely explanation is that the cement barrier has failed. If we displace the mud, nothing stands between this rig and a blowout. We cannot explain the readings with a benign cause, and the consequence of being wrong is a well control event that risks the rig and the crew." The third operation is delivering the consequence rather than the mechanism. The well site leaders did not need to understand kill-line hydraulics or bladder effects. They needed to understand that the proceed decision was being made with evidence suggesting the primary barrier had failed, and that the consequence of a wrong call was not a delay but a potential loss of the rig and its crew. The engineers had all the information necessary to make this translation. The translation was never performed, and eleven people died. The gap between what the engineers knew and what the decision-makers heard was not a knowledge gap. It was a framing gap, and closing it was the engineers' responsibility, because they were the ones who understood both the data and its implications.

· · ·

The distinction between "you problems" and "them problems" is a framework for performing this translation, and it is worth defining with precision because the terminology suggests a cynicism that is not present in the actual practice.

A "you problem" is a concern expressed in the speaker's own frame, using the speaker's own vocabulary, motivated by the speaker's own priorities. "It won't be maintainable" is a you problem when spoken by an engineer to a product manager under deadline pressure, because maintainability is an engineering concern that lives in the engineer's world, not the product manager's. "The test coverage is below eighty percent" is a you problem when spoken to an executive who does not know what test coverage means. "The architecture is not scalable" is a you problem when spoken to a customer who needs the system to work today and does not care whether it scales tomorrow. The front-end lead in the coaching session listed nine or ten technical constraints explaining why a proposed implementation was problematic. The product team heard a list of reasons the engineer did not want to do the work.

A "them problem" is the same concern, translated into the listener's frame, expressed in the listener's vocabulary, and connected to the listener's priorities. "If we do this, these other features you want won't happen" is a them problem for a product manager, because feature delivery against the roadmap is what the product manager is evaluated on. "Every week of delay increases the probability of a production incident that will require all-hands response and delay the Q2 roadmap" is a them problem for an executive. "This configuration means your reports may fail during your busiest period" is a them problem for a customer.

The objection to this framework, which the front-end lead raised directly in the coaching session, is that it sounds manipulative. The concern is legitimate and worth addressing head-on, because the framework's value depends on understanding why it is not manipulation. Manipulation distorts the message to produce a desired response. Translation preserves the message while changing the encoding. The architectural constraints are real. The roadmap delays are consequences of the architectural constraints. The engineer who presents the roadmap delays is not inventing a concern to frighten the product manager into approving the refactoring. The engineer is presenting the actual consequence of the technical problem, expressed in the terms that allow the product manager to evaluate it alongside the other priorities competing for the same resources. As the coach framed it: adapting your communication to the mental state of the person you are talking to is no different from adjusting your conversation when a friend has had a terrible day. You are not manipulating them. You are acknowledging where they are so that the conversation can be productive. The product manager may still decline the refactoring, because the enterprise contract renewals may genuinely be more important than the roadmap risk. That is a legitimate business decision, and it is a decision the product manager can only make correctly if the engineer has presented the relevant information in a form the product manager can process.

• • •

Crawford-Sobel's theory of hierarchical information degradation applies here in a different and more practical way. Crawford-Sobel predicts that information degrades in transmission when the sender and receiver have different incentive functions. The engineer and the product director have different incentive functions: the engineer is incentivized to maintain system health, the product director is incentivized to deliver features that generate revenue. These incentives are not contradictory (both parties want the system to work and the business to succeed), but they are different enough that a message optimized for the engineer's frame will be received with degradation in the product director's frame.

The translation skill is the engineering discipline of minimizing Crawford-Sobel degradation in human communication. You cannot eliminate the degradation, because you cannot eliminate the incentive difference that causes it. You can minimize it by encoding the message in the receiver's frame, so that the message is processed against the receiver's incentive function rather than against the gap between the sender's incentive function and the receiver's. The product director who hears "connection pool exhaustion" processes the message through a filter that says "I don't know how to evaluate this, so I'll default to my existing priorities." The product director who hears "sixty percent probability of SLA-violating outage" processes the message through a filter that says "I know exactly how to evaluate this, and it changes my priority calculation." The information is the same. The encoding determines whether the information survives the transmission.

The 100/100 principle provides the operational test for whether the translation has been performed correctly. The principle states that a fully competent engineer and a fully competent business stakeholder, both operating in good faith with full information, should reach the same decision about a technical investment. If they disagree, the disagreement is evidence that one of them is operating with incomplete information: either the engineer does not understand the business constraints, or the stakeholder does not understand the technical risk. The 100/100 principle does not say who is right. It says that disagreement between competent, well-informed people indicates a communication failure, and the communication failure is the engineer's responsibility to diagnose and repair, because the engineer is the one who holds the technical information and therefore the one who must perform the translation.

• • •

The application to AI-assisted development is direct. When code is cheap, the engineer's time shifts from production to specification and verification. Specification requires understanding what the business needs, which requires communicating with people who understand the business and who express their understanding in business terms. Verification requires understanding what "correct" means in context, which frequently requires understanding the business rules, the regulatory requirements, and the user expectations that define correctness for this specific system. Every one of these understanding tasks is a translation task: taking information from one frame, processing it for its essential content, and re-encoding it in a form that allows the engineer to act on it.

The engineer who cannot perform this translation is reduced to implementing specifications written by other people, and an engineer who implements specifications written by other people is competing directly with AI, which implements specifications faster, cheaper, and, increasingly, with comparable quality. The engineer who can perform the translation is doing work that AI cannot currently do and that the information-theoretic constraints of human communication suggest will be resistant to automation for some time: the extraction of tacit, contextual, incentive-laden information from human stakeholders through conversation, and the integration of that information into technical specifications that accurately capture what the stakeholders actually need rather than what they said they wanted.

This is not a comfortable position for engineers who entered the field because they preferred interacting with machines rather than with people. The discomfort is real and worth acknowledging. The economics are also real and not negotiable: when machines can write the code, the engineer's value is determined by the quality of the specification, and the quality of the specification is determined by the quality of the communication between the engineer and the people who know what the specification should say. The engineer who retreats into the technical frame, speaking only in the terms of their own expertise and leaving the translation to "the business side," has ceded the most valuable part of their role to someone who may or may not have the technical understanding to fill it.

• • •

The skill is learnable, which is worth stating explicitly because the industry's treatment of communication skills as innate personality traits rather than acquired competencies has produced a generation of engineers who believe they either have the skill or do not and there is nothing to be done about it.

The practice begins with a question that most engineers skip: what is the listener's frame? What do they care about? What vocabulary do they use? What incentives govern their decisions? These are empirical questions with observable answers. The product manager who talks about roadmap velocity, feature delivery, and client satisfaction cares about roadmap velocity, feature delivery, and client satisfaction. The executive who talks about headcount, runway, and market position cares about headcount, runway, and market position. The customer who talks about report accuracy, export speed, and quarterly deadlines cares about report accuracy, export speed, and quarterly deadlines. The information is available to any engineer who listens for it, and listening for it is the first step in the translation.

The second step is the mapping: for each technical concern, identify the consequence that lives in the listener's frame. Technical debt maps to increased development time, which maps to delayed feature delivery, which maps to missed revenue targets. Security vulnerability maps to data breach risk, which maps to regulatory penalty, which maps to customer trust erosion. An incomplete migration maps to rework, which maps to slower feature velocity, which maps to missed quarterly targets. The mapping is not always straightforward, and there are technical concerns that do not have clear business consequences, which is useful information: a concern with no business consequence may not be worth raising, and the exercise of attempting the mapping forces the engineer to examine whether the concern is genuinely important or merely interesting.

To make the operation concrete, consider a worked example from the coaching sessions. An engineer's team is asked to rush a major design system migration. The engineer's instinct is to present the technical case: the existing codebase has architectural constraints that the new design must respect, the components are interdependent in ways that the design team does not understand, and a rushed implementation will produce code that must be rewritten when server-side rendering is added the following month. All of this is true. All of it is a "you problem." The mapping proceeds: rushed implementation means rework next month, rework next month means the features the product team wants in Q2 are delayed, delayed Q2 features mean the company's metrics suffer heading into a funding round that depends on demonstrated product velocity. The delivery: "If we rush the migration, the SSR work next month will force us to rebuild what we just shipped. The features you need for the funding timeline get pushed back by the rework. Taking an extra two weeks now eliminates the rework and keeps the Q2 roadmap intact." The product manager now has a decision framed in terms they evaluate daily: funding timeline, Q2 roadmap, feature velocity. The technical content has not changed. The encoding has.

The third step is the delivery, and the delivery is the simplest part because, by this point, the engineer knows what to say and how to say it. Lead with the consequence rather than the cause, frame the risk in terms the listener can evaluate without understanding the mechanism, and give them a decision to make rather than a diagnosis to absorb. The product manager does not need to understand the component architecture. The product manager needs to understand that there is a quantifiable risk to the roadmap, that the risk can be mitigated at a known cost, and that the decision is theirs to make with full information. The engineer's job is to ensure that the information is full. The decision is someone else's.

This division of responsibility, the engineer provides the information, the stakeholder makes the decision, is not a subordination of engineering to business. It is a partnership in which each party contributes what they are best positioned to contribute, and the quality of the partnership depends on the quality of the information transfer. The engineer who provides information in a form the stakeholder cannot process has failed the partnership as surely as the stakeholder who makes decisions without consulting the engineer. Translation is the engineer's half of that contract, and in a world where the other half of the engineer's traditional contribution (writing the code) is increasingly automated, it may be the half that matters most.

CHAPTER 15

Organizational Navigation

A senior engineering lead at a growth-stage company is responsible for code review on a major product. The reviews typically take one day, sometimes less. The product team, under pressure to deliver features before a funding round, begins treating the reviews as a bottleneck. Stakeholders start bypassing the lead by messaging junior engineers directly, asking them to merge changes without review. The lead raises the concern: reviews are how the team catches architectural regressions, and skipping them during a migration to a new design system is precisely the moment when the risk is highest. The product team hears an engineer who is slowing them down. The lead knows, with the confidence of someone who has seen the bugs that reviews catch, that bypassing the process will increase the defect rate. The lead also knows that the product team's pressure is not irrational: they are optimizing for delivery velocity because the CEO evaluates the product organization on features shipped, and the funding round depends on demonstrating product momentum. The lead is caught between a technical reality (reviews prevent defects) and an organizational reality (the product team's incentive structure rewards speed over safety), and the resolution of the conflict depends not on who is technically correct but on the lead's ability to navigate the organizational structure that produced the conflict.

This situation is not unusual. Some version of it occurs in every engineering organization, at every scale, with sufficient regularity that it should be understood as a structural property of organizations rather than as an individual misfortune. The engineer who treats it as an aberration, as a case of bad management to be endured or escaped, will encounter it again at the next company, because the forces that produce it are not specific to any company. They are properties of hierarchical coordination operating under Goodhart's Law, and they are as predictable as hierarchical information degradation.

• • •

The forces that govern organizations are structural, not personal, and understanding this distinction is the prerequisite for navigating them. When the product team bypasses the code review process, the natural human response is to interpret the behavior as a judgment about the engineering lead's priorities: the product team does not value quality, does not understand engineering, is behaving irresponsibly. These interpretations may or may not be accurate descriptions of any individual, but they are irrelevant to the engineer's ability to navigate the situation, because the situation would exist regardless of who occupied the product roles. Any product manager evaluated on feature delivery velocity will face pressure to remove obstacles to delivery velocity. The pressure is a property of the incentive structure, not a property of the person. Replace the product manager with a better product manager, and the new product manager will face the same pressure, interpret it through their own judgment, and arrive at a decision that is shaped by the same structural force.

This is the concept that the author's previous work, *The Cage and the Mirror*, examined in detail: the cage of structural forces that constrain individual action in organizations. The cage is not built by anyone. It is not maintained by anyone. It is an emergent property of the interaction between hierarchical compression, incentive misalignment, and proxy optimization, the same forces that the Chapter 2 experiments demonstrated in a system with no humans at all. An architecture that incentivized rejection produced rejection regardless of the work's quality — no human ego involved, just structural incentive operating through pure mathematics. The product manager who circumvents the review process is responding to an analogous incentive, created by an analogous architecture, with analogous consequences. The physics is the same.

Understanding that the forces are structural rather than personal does not make them less powerful. It makes them navigable, in the way that understanding the physics of an ocean current makes the current navigable even though it does not make the current weaker. The engineer who attributes the product team's behavior to personal failure will respond with frustration, resentment, or resignation, none of which changes the structural force. The engineer who recognizes the structural force can work with it: demonstrating that reviews catch regressions that would require more time to fix in production than the one-day review costs, establishing clear authority over the review process so that bypass attempts are redirected rather than accommodated, or surfacing the trade-off in terms that allow the product team to make an informed decision rather than a pressured one. These are navigational moves, not confrontational ones, and they work because they address the structure rather than the person.

• • •

Perspective shifting is the cognitive operation that makes organizational navigation possible, and it is the same operation that underlies effective technical-to-business translation. The engineer who can see the situation from the product team's perspective, who can understand why delivery velocity is the metric being optimized and what pressures the product managers face from above, can craft a response that accounts for those constraints rather than ignoring them. The response is not appeasement. It is engineering applied to an organizational problem: understanding the constraints, identifying the degrees of freedom, and designing a solution that satisfies the technical requirement within the organizational constraints.

The practice of perspective shifting is more rigorous than the phrase suggests. It is not empathy in the colloquial sense of feeling what someone else feels. It is the construction of a model of another person's decision-making process: what information they have, what incentives they operate under, what constraints they face, what outcomes they are optimizing for. This model is built the same way any model is built: through observation, hypothesis, and testing. You observe a product manager's behavior across multiple situations. You form a hypothesis about the incentive structure that produces that behavior. You test the hypothesis by predicting what the product manager will do in a new situation and comparing the prediction to the actual response. When the predictions are consistently accurate, you have a working model of their decision process, and you can use that model to design communications and proposals that are compatible with their frame.

This is the scientific method applied to organizational dynamics, and it is as far from the soft-skill characterization as it is possible to be. A scientist models a physical system by observing its behavior, hypothesizing about the forces that produce the behavior, and testing the hypothesis with predictions. An engineer who models an organizational system is doing the same thing, and the accuracy of the model determines the effectiveness of the navigation. The engineer whose model of the product manager is "doesn't care about quality" will make predictions that are wrong whenever the product manager does care about quality (which is most of the time; the concern about delivery velocity is not indifference to quality but optimization of a different proxy). The engineer whose model is "optimizes for delivery velocity because that is the metric leadership uses to evaluate the product organization, especially heading into a funding round" will make predictions that are correct across a wider range of situations, because the model captures the structural force rather than imputing a personal motivation.

• • •

There are patterns of organizational navigation that recur across organizations and that are worth naming, because naming them makes them visible and visibility is the prerequisite for deliberate use.

The first is the use of past predictions to build credibility. In a coaching session, a director of engineering described making an explicit prediction to leadership: if the company compressed a nine-month project into six weeks, the team would ship a broken product, immediately begin firefighting customer complaints, and never circle back to build the testing and reliability infrastructure that the compressed timeline had eliminated. Leadership chose speed. Within weeks, the product was live, customers were complaining, and the team was refactoring an unfinished system while simultaneously onboarding new clients. When leadership later asked why there were no tests, the director's response was precise: "Tests are what you get when you do a nine-month project in nine months. When you do it in six weeks, you don't get tests. You made that decision. Don't be upset with the team for giving you what you asked for." The prediction had been stated in advance, the outcome was observable, and the engineer's credibility on subsequent resource-allocation decisions was measurably higher because the evidence was not debatable. This is not the vindictive "I told you so" that organizations punish. It is the accumulation of a track record that makes subsequent predictions more credible, because the predictions are grounded in a demonstrated understanding of the system's behavior. The engineer who tracks their predictions and their outcomes is doing science: forming hypotheses, testing them against reality, and using the results to calibrate future hypotheses.

The second pattern is the protection of people who do not know to say no. Junior engineers, new hires, and engineers in vulnerable positions are frequently asked to take on work that is unreasonable, not because anyone intends to exploit them but because the organizational structure does not have a mechanism for distinguishing between a reasonable request and an unreasonable one. In the coaching sessions, the director described the dynamic with directness: "Junior engineers have no clue. They say yes because someone asked." When a stakeholder bypasses the lead and messages a junior engineer directly, asking them to merge changes without review, the junior complies because the request came from someone they perceive as having authority, and they lack the organizational model to recognize that the request violates the process their lead established. The senior engineer who recognizes this dynamic and intervenes, not by criticizing the person making the request but by surfacing the constraint that makes the request unreasonable, is navigating the organizational structure on behalf of someone who cannot navigate it themselves. In the coaching transcript, the lead was instructed to tell his engineers explicitly: if someone asks you to circumvent the process, come to me first, because I can help you do it correctly, and if you do it the other way, I will block the review. The instruction is not punitive. It gives the junior engineer a structural mechanism for saying no: they can point to the lead's authority rather than having to assert their own, which they do not yet have. The intervention works because it addresses the structural vulnerability (the junior has no mechanism for refusing) rather than the personal one (the junior is too agreeable).

The third pattern is radical candor that focuses on growth rather than on judgment. The phrase "radical candor" has been diluted by popular use into a license for blunt feedback, which is not what it means in practice. Effective candor is specific, timely, and oriented toward a concrete behavior that the recipient can change. "Your code reviews are too slow" is judgment. "Your reviews on the payment service are blocking the release cycle. If you focus each review on the logic and security passes and defer the style concerns to the linter, the review time would drop without reducing the quality of the feedback" is candor. The first statement tells the recipient they are doing something wrong. The second shows the recipient how to do something differently, with enough specificity that the change is actionable and enough context that the reasoning is transparent. The difference is the difference between evaluating the person and engineering the behavior.

• • •

The organizational landscape has a feature that the technical landscape does not, and it is worth naming because it is the trap that catches the most talented navigators. The technical landscape rewards understanding: the engineer who understands the system's physics can predict its behavior and design solutions that work. The organizational landscape also rewards understanding, but it additionally rewards certain forms of behavior that are not connected to understanding and that can substitute for it in the short term. Political skill, the ability to accumulate and deploy social capital, can produce organizational outcomes that are independent of technical merit. The engineer who navigates organizations effectively will, at some point, discover that the navigational skills they have developed are also usable as political skills, and the temptation to deploy them politically rather than structurally is considerable, because political deployment is faster and its results are more immediately visible.

This is the patrimonial trap: the discovery that you can use organizational understanding to accumulate personal power rather than to solve organizational problems, and the progressive substitution of the former for the latter. The trap is gradual, and its gradualness is what makes it dangerous, because the engineer in the middle of the drift does not experience it as a drift.

Consider what the progression looks like from the inside. An architect at a mid-sized company develops a sophisticated model of the organizational dynamics: who controls budget, whose opinion the CTO trusts, which teams have political capital and which do not. The architect uses this understanding structurally at first, routing proposals through the people most likely to evaluate them on merit, timing technical recommendations to coincide with budget cycles when investment decisions are made, framing infrastructure work in terms that the finance-minded COO can evaluate. These are navigational moves, and they produce good outcomes. The architect's proposals get funded. The systems improve. The architect's reputation grows. At some point, the architect begins to notice that the model is useful for things beyond system health. The architect can predict which projects will receive executive attention and position themselves on those projects. The architect can identify which engineers are likely to be promoted and cultivate relationships with them early. The architect can sense when a reorganization is coming and pre-position their team to absorb the most desirable projects. None of these moves are malicious. Each one, individually, is reasonable career management. The drift is in the aggregate: the architect's organizational model, which was built to navigate structural forces in service of system health, is now being used primarily to navigate structural forces in service of the architect's career. The system health benefits have become incidental. From the outside, the signs are legible to anyone who knows what to look for. The architect's technical recommendations increasingly align with their political interests. Proposals that would benefit the system but reduce the architect's scope never get made. Engineers who might challenge the architect's technical authority are subtly excluded from key decisions. The architect still speaks the language of engineering, still frames decisions in terms of system health, still presents evidence and makes predictions, but the predictions have become unfalsifiable because the architect now has enough political capital to ensure that their preferred outcomes materialize regardless of the technical merits. The track record looks impressive. The system is quietly degrading.

The progression is visible in practice. A senior technical leader joins a company and develops a genuine structural insight: information is flowing around certain roles, decisions are being made outside their designated channels, authority does not match title in several parts of the organization. The leader uses this insight structurally at first, routing technical recommendations through the people whose authority matches the decision, identifying where a director's span of control has outgrown the reporting structure, surfacing the gap between the org chart and the actual communication topology. The recommendations are good. They improve the system. The leader's credibility rises, which is when the drift begins. The leader starts positioning themselves on high-visibility projects before the projects are announced, cultivating relationships with people who hold informal power rather than formal authority, pre-empting reorganizations by moving political allies into positions that will survive the restructure. Each move, taken individually, looks like reasonable organizational awareness. Taken as a trajectory, the pattern is legible: the leader's recommendations begin aligning with their political interests rather than with system health. A proposal to consolidate two teams under a single architect would improve coordination, but the leader does not make it, because the consolidation would reduce the leader's scope. A recommendation to promote a strong technical contributor is deferred, because the contributor has publicly disagreed with the leader's architectural direction. The leader still speaks in the language of system health, still presents evidence, still makes predictions, but the evidence has become selective and the predictions have become unfalsifiable. The structural insight that once served the organization now serves the leader's position within it, and the transition happened so gradually that the leader may not recognize it has occurred.

This progression is Diane Vaughan's normalized deviance applied to an individual's organizational navigation rather than to an organization's safety standards. Each small political move is individually reasonable, the drift is incremental, and success breeds the confidence that enables the next deviation. The defense against it is the same defense Vaughan's work implies for organizations: transparency that makes the drift visible, evidence that can be evaluated independently, and falsifiability that prevents the navigator from insulating their conclusions from disconfirmation.

The defense against the patrimonial trap is scientific discipline: transparency, falsifiability, and accountability to evidence. The engineer who navigates organizations by making predictions and tracking their accuracy is constrained by the evidence. The predictions are public. The outcomes are observable. The track record is falsifiable. This discipline prevents the drift from structural navigation to political manipulation, because manipulation depends on opacity (the manipulator's model of the system is private, and their predictions are unfalsifiable because they are never stated explicitly), while navigation depends on transparency (the navigator's predictions are stated, tested, and revised). The diagnostic is whether you take actions that benefit the system but cost you politically. The engineer who consistently does is navigating. The engineer who has stopped encountering the question has drifted.

• • •

The AI age does not diminish the importance of organizational navigation. If anything, it amplifies the importance, because the decisions that determine whether AI tools help or hurt an engineering organization are organizational decisions, not technical ones. Whether to invest in context engineering or to let developers vibe-code. Whether to implement mechanical verification or to rely on advisory review. Whether to allocate time for engineers to develop understanding or to optimize for feature velocity. Each of these decisions is made within an organizational structure governed by incentive structures, proxy metrics, and hierarchical compression, and the engineer who cannot navigate that structure cannot influence those decisions, regardless of how well the engineer understands the technical merits.

The engineer who understands the physics, the information theory, the coordination costs, the constraint topology, the cognitive science, the Goodhart dynamics, has a necessary but insufficient foundation. The physics must be translated into the organizational frame, which requires the skill of translating between technical and business reality. It must be deployed within the organizational structure, which requires navigational skill. And it must be maintained against the organizational pressures that favor short-term metrics over long-term system health, which requires the credibility, the perspective-shifting ability, and the structural awareness that organizational navigation demands.

The engineers on the Deepwater Horizon spent over an hour debating anomalous pressure readings. They did not lack technical understanding. They did not lack data. They lacked the organizational navigation to translate what they knew into a form that the decision-makers could act on, within a structure whose incentives — a million dollars per day in rig costs, a project already behind schedule — were aligned against the action the data recommended. The physics of the well blowout was straightforward. The physics of the organizational failure was the same: structural forces, incentive misalignment, proxy optimization, and the compression of high-fidelity technical information into a decision frame that could not accommodate it. The engineering lead protecting code reviews at a startup and the drilling engineer questioning a pressure test on a deepwater rig are navigating the same forces at different scales, with different stakes, but with the same underlying requirement: understand the structure, model the incentives, translate the concern, and make the prediction public so that the evidence, not the economics, determines what happens next.

PART VI

The Future

CHAPTER 16

What Engineers Become

There is a job title that has circulated in the industry since 2023, "prompt engineer," that captured the imagination of recruiters, career coaches, and career-advice commentators before quietly fading from serious engineering discourse. The trajectory of the title is instructive. Indeed reported that searches for "prompt engineer" surged from two per million total U.S. job searches in January 2023 to 144 per million by April of that year, then collapsed to a plateau of twenty to thirty per million, where they have remained. An analysis of LinkedIn job postings found seventy-two prompt engineer positions out of more than twenty thousand AI-related postings, representing 0.35 percent of the AI job market. A Microsoft-commissioned survey ranked "prompt engineer" second to last among new roles companies were considering adding. An entire job title created, evangelized, hired for, and abandoned in less time than a typical performance improvement plan takes to complete. The title was a misdiagnosis. It identified the surface symptom, the interaction with AI through natural language prompts, and elevated it to a role, in the way that calling a civil engineer a "concrete pourer" would elevate one physical activity to a profession while missing everything that makes the profession a profession. The people who were actually good at getting AI to produce useful output were not people who had mastered the art of prompt construction. They were experienced engineers who understood the systems they were building and who used that understanding to construct information environments in which the AI's output was constrained by reality rather than by the model's training distribution. The skill was not prompting. The skill was engineering, applied to a new medium.

This distinction matters because it determines what engineers need to learn and what they can safely ignore. The engineer who invests in learning "prompt tricks," the specific phrasings, persona definitions, and output-formatting instructions that produce marginally better results from current models, is investing in knowledge that will be obsolete within one product cycle, because the specific tricks that work on today's models will not work on tomorrow's models, and the tricks are not grounded in any transferable understanding of why they work. The engineer who invests in understanding the physics, the information theory, the coordination dynamics, the constraint design, the cognitive science, is investing in knowledge that will transfer to whatever tools and architectures emerge next, because the physics does not change when the tools change.

• • •

The role that is emerging is better understood as three distinct competencies that were always present in strong engineering practice but that were partially obscured by the mechanical labor of code production.

Context engineering, the construction of information environments that produce accurate output from whatever agent operates within them, is the most immediately recognizable of the three. It applies identically to human agents and artificial ones. The engineer who constructs a good onboarding experience for a new team member is doing context engineering. The engineer who writes a CLAUDE.md file that captures the project's architectural constraints and naming conventions is doing context engineering. The engineer who designs a knowledge base that allows a customer support system to answer questions accurately is doing context engineering. The medium varies; the competency is the same: understanding what information an agent needs to operate effectively, providing that information in a form the agent can process, and excluding the information that would degrade the agent's performance.

Constraint design operates at a different level: the specification of the boundaries within which work must occur, expressed as mechanical, enforceable, automatically verified conditions rather than as guidelines, preferences, or suggestions. The engineer who designs a test suite that captures the system's required behaviors is doing constraint design. The engineer who configures a CI pipeline that blocks deployment on security violations is doing constraint design. The engineer who specifies the interface contracts between microservices in a form that can be mechanically verified at integration time is doing constraint design. The output of constraint design is not code. It is the shape that code must fit, and the shape is more durable than any individual implementation that fills it.

Where constraint design shapes the boundaries of individual work, coordination architecture addresses the connections between workers: the design of the mechanisms through which multiple agents, human or artificial, coordinate their work without losing the information that coordination requires. The engineer who chooses between stigmergic coordination and hierarchical delegation for a particular task decomposition is doing coordination architecture. The engineer who designs the shared environment through which a multi-agent system communicates is doing coordination architecture. The engineer who recognizes that a particular task should not be distributed at all, because the information loss of distribution exceeds the benefit of parallelism, is doing coordination architecture. The output of coordination architecture is not code. It is the topology of information flow that determines whether the code produced by multiple agents will compose into a functioning system.

These competencies are abstract in description. They are concrete in practice. Consider what a senior engineer exercising coordination architecture actually does on a given afternoon. A product team requests a new feature that touches three services owned by three different teams. The coordination architect does not write the code for any of the services. The architect examines the interfaces between them: what data crosses the boundaries, what assumptions each service makes about the others' behavior, what happens when one service deploys a change before the others are ready. The architect discovers that two of the services share an implicit assumption about the format of a timestamp field, undocumented and unenforced. The architect writes a contract test that makes the assumption explicit and mechanical, so that a change to the format in one service will fail the contract check before it reaches production. The architect then considers the deployment sequence: service A must deploy before service B because B depends on a new endpoint in A, but service C can deploy independently. The architect documents this ordering in the shared environment (a deployment manifest, a CLAUDE.md file, a Pact contract), so that any agent, human or AI, that attempts to deploy C before A will be stopped by the constraint rather than discovered by the incident. The afternoon's work produced no feature code. It produced the conditions under which the feature code, written by three teams or three AI agents, will compose into a working system rather than a set of individually correct but collectively broken components.

• • •

These three competencies were always the substance of senior engineering. A principal engineer at a large technology company has always spent the majority of their time on context (ensuring that teams have the information they need), constraints (defining the architectural standards that keep a large system coherent), and coordination (designing the interactions between teams and services so that the overall system works). The principal engineer's job was never to write the most code. It was to create the conditions under which good code was produced by others. The fact that "others" now includes AI agents does not change the job description. It changes the scale at which the job operates, because AI agents can produce code faster than humans, which means the conditions that govern that production become proportionally more important.

The career ladder that emerges from this understanding is not unfamiliar. It is the career ladder that has always existed in engineering, stripped of the confusion that code production introduced. A junior engineer learns to write code that works. At the mid-level, the scope widens to writing code that works within a system, which requires understanding the system's constraints and conventions. Senior engineers take ownership of the constraints and conventions themselves, designing them so that other engineers' code works within the system. At the principal or staff level, the responsibility extends to the coordination architecture that connects multiple systems, teams, and stakeholders into a coherent whole. At each level, the scope of the engineer's responsibility expands from the implementation to the environment in which the implementation occurs, and the nature of the contribution shifts from producing artifacts to producing the conditions that make good artifacts possible.

The AI transition accelerates this progression without changing its nature. A junior engineer who uses AI tools effectively is a junior engineer who learns faster, because the tools handle the mechanical labor of syntax and library calls while the engineer focuses on understanding the system. A senior engineer who uses AI tools effectively is a senior engineer who operates at greater scale, because the tools handle the implementation of individual components while the engineer focuses on the context, constraints, and coordination that make the components compose. The tools do not create a new career path. They reveal the career path that was always there, by removing the mechanical labor that obscured it.

• • •

The concept of the epistemological gate deserves explicit treatment, because it names a function that is becoming increasingly important as AI capabilities expand and that is difficult to automate for reasons that are structural rather than technological.

An epistemological gate is a point in a process where someone must determine whether an artifact, a specification, a piece of code, a test suite, a deployment, is correct. "Correct" in this context does not mean "syntactically valid" or "compiles without errors" or "passes the existing tests." It means "does what it is supposed to do, in the context of the actual requirements, for the actual users, under the actual conditions of production." This determination requires knowledge that is distributed across multiple sources: the business requirements (which live in the product team's heads), the technical constraints (which live in the codebase and the infrastructure), the user expectations (which live in support tickets and usage data), and the operational context (which lives in the incident history and the monitoring dashboards). No single artifact contains all of this knowledge. No single model has access to all of this knowledge. The person who stands at the epistemological gate, who synthesizes these inputs and renders a judgment about whether the artifact is correct, is performing a function that requires access to information that is dispersed, tacit, contextual, and frequently contradictory.

AI can assist at the epistemological gate. It can run the tests, verify the types, check the contracts, flag potential issues, and produce a report that summarizes the mechanical verification results. What it cannot do, given the current state of the technology and the information-theoretic constraints on what any model can access, is determine whether the tests themselves are correct, whether the contracts capture the actual requirements, whether the mechanical verification covers the cases that matter, and whether the artifact will behave correctly in the specific production environment with its specific data, its specific traffic patterns, and its specific failure modes. These determinations require the kind of contextual, synthesized judgment that constitutes grokking: the generative understanding of the system that produces predictions about novel situations, as opposed to the pattern matching that produces correct behavior in familiar ones.

The engineer who functions as an effective epistemological gate is the engineer who has grokked the system: who has built, through sustained engagement with the system's complexity, a mental model of the system that generates accurate predictions about its behavior under conditions that were not explicitly specified. This engineer is not replaceable by a checklist, because the value of their judgment lies precisely in the cases that no checklist anticipated. They are the person who looks at a deployment that passes all tests and says "this will fail in production because the test environment does not replicate the connection pool contention that occurs under peak load," and they say this not because there is a test for connection pool contention (there is not) but because their mental model of the system includes the production environment's behavior under load, and their model generates the prediction that no existing test captures.

• • •

Will the epistemological gate remain human? The honest answer is that the boundary between what can and cannot be automated is not stable. Capabilities that seemed permanently beyond AI's reach five years ago are routine today. Predictions about what will remain human tend to be overtaken by developments that the predictions did not anticipate.

What does not change is the need for the function. Regardless of whether the function is performed by a human or by an AI system, someone or something must determine whether the artifact is correct in the full, contextual, business-aware sense of "correct." The physics of the specification gap, the permanent distance between what someone wants and what they can articulate, guarantees that mechanical verification alone will never be sufficient, because the tests can only verify what was specified, and the specification is always incomplete. The gap must be filled by judgment, and the quality of the judgment depends on the depth of understanding that the judge has of the system, its context, and its purpose.

The engineer who develops this understanding, who invests in grokking rather than in surface-level familiarity, who builds the associative web of cross-contextual knowledge that grokking produces, is developing the competency that the function requires regardless of who performs it. If the function remains human, the engineer is the person who performs it. If the function is automated, the engineer is the person who designs the system that performs it, because designing such a system requires understanding what the function actually does, and understanding what the function does is precisely what the engineer's deep engagement has produced. The understanding transfers. The specific role may not.

• • •

The scientist-engineer is not a new profession. It is the oldest profession in engineering, predating the specializations, the framework wars, the certification programs, and the tribal loyalties that the industry accumulated during the decades when code was expensive and experimentation was prohibitive. When code is cheap and experimentation is accessible, the engineer who experiments, measures, and reasons from evidence has an advantage that no amount of tribal loyalty or framework familiarity can match, because the advantage is grounded in the dynamics of the problem rather than in the conventions of the current solution.

The physicist does not memorize the trajectory of every projectile. The physicist understands the forces that govern all projectiles, and derives the specific trajectory from the specific initial conditions. The engineer who has absorbed the physics, the information theory, the coordination dynamics, the constraint design, the cognitive science, the Goodhart traps, the organizational forces, does not need to memorize the practices that work for current tools. The practices are consequences of the structural forces, and the engineer can derive the appropriate practice for any new tool from the physics that governs all tools. This is what it means to understand rather than to know, and it is the difference between an engineer who will navigate the transition and an engineer who will be navigated by it.

The "prompt engineer" title peaked and collapsed in under eighteen months. The competencies it gestured toward, context engineering, constraint design, and coordination architecture, are decades old and will outlast whatever title the industry invents next. The engineer who builds a career on titles is building on the same foundation as the engineer who builds a career on a specific framework: the foundation is the current convention, and conventions change. The engineer who builds a career on the physics is building on the forces that generate the conventions, and those forces do not have release cycles.

Chapter 17

What We Build Next

In the time it took you to read this book, the landscape changed. That sentence is not a rhetorical device. The rate of change in AI capability follows what researchers have begun to call the Densing Law, documented in Nature Machine Intelligence in 2025: capability per parameter doubles approximately every three and a half months. The cost of frontier reasoning models collapsed by a factor of twenty-seven in a single generation (from roughly fifteen dollars per million input tokens to fifty-five cents). The model that produced the dysfunction experiments is already slower, smaller, and less capable than the model available as you read this sentence. The context windows once described as finite and precious have expanded to one million tokens in production models. The coordination architectures that failed at scale are being re-implemented with each new generation of capability, and some of the failure modes documented earlier have already been partially addressed by improvements in the underlying models. The specific findings will age. The physics will not.

The Densing Law implies two questions worth examining separately: the trajectory of what is changing, extrapolated from the rate of change rather than from the current state, and the invariants that do not change regardless of what the trajectory produces. The trajectory tells you what is coming. The invariants tell you what to do about it.

The trajectory is most visible in the tasks that have already migrated from human to automated execution, because the migration pattern reveals the sequence in which subsequent tasks will follow. The sequence is not random. It is governed by two properties of each task: the clarity of its specification and the mechanizability of its verification. Tasks that score high on both migrate first. Tasks that score low on both migrate last. The ordering is predictable even when the specific timeline is not.

Code generation was the first task to migrate, and it migrated so quickly that the industry barely registered the transition as a transition. Within eighteen months of the first competent code-generation tools, the question shifted from "can AI write code?" to "how do we manage the code AI writes?" Generation was the easiest task to automate because it has the clearest specification: here is a description of what the function should do, produce the function. The specification is the input. The code is the output. The mapping between them is well-defined enough that a language model trained on hundreds of billions of tokens of existing code can produce the output with reasonable accuracy for a wide range of inputs.

Testing migrated next. AI systems that can generate code can also generate test cases, because test generation is structurally similar to code generation: here is a specification of the expected behavior, produce code that verifies the behavior. The quality of AI-generated tests is variable, and the familiar failure modes apply with full force (a test suite optimized by a model that is rewarded for coverage will produce coverage theater), but the mechanical generation of test scaffolding, the boilerplate of test setup, assertion structure, and edge case enumeration, is no longer a human task in organizations that have adopted the tools.

The next migration in progress is what might be called the death of maintenance. Maintenance, in the traditional sense, is the process of detecting a defect in a running system, diagnosing its cause, designing a fix, implementing the fix, testing the fix, and deploying the fix. Each of these steps is becoming automated, not as a speculative future but as an engineering reality in systems that are currently operating. A monitoring system detects a fault. The fault is diagnosed by an AI agent that examines the error logs, the stack trace, and the recent changes to the codebase. The diagnosis identifies the component that is failing. The agent generates a new test suite that captures the failure: a set of tests that the current implementation fails and that any correct implementation must pass. The agent then generates a new implementation of the component, one that satisfies all the original tests (the behavior the component was supposed to exhibit before the failure) plus the new tests (the behavior the failure revealed was missing). The new implementation is deployed through a staging environment where it must pass the full test suite before reaching production. The failing component is not patched. It is replaced, entirely, with a new component that does everything the old component did plus the thing the old component failed to do.

This loop, detect, diagnose, specify, replace, verify, promote, is not hypothetical. The individual steps exist in current tooling. The integration of those steps into a closed loop is engineering work that is actively underway, and the information-theoretic constraints that might prevent its completion are not evident. Meta's WhatsApp engineering team documented a twenty-five-month deployment of AI-assisted code generation that processed more than three thousand accepted code changes, and the stable operating pattern that emerged is revealing: sixty percent of changes were accepted with a single click, while forty percent required human guidance. That ratio stabilized over time, meaning it is not a transitional state converging toward full automation but an equilibrium reflecting the boundary between tasks the AI handles well and tasks that still require human judgment. The sixty percent is the auto-remediation loop in nascent form: well-specified changes with mechanical verification, executed without human intervention. The forty percent is the specification gap, the contextual judgment, the tacit knowledge that is the engineer's enduring contribution.

Each step in the loop is a well-defined task with a clear specification and verifiable output, which is the profile of tasks that AI handles well. The coordination between steps is sequential rather than parallel, which means the information loss that plagued the multi-agent architectures is minimized. The verification at each step is mechanical rather than advisory, which means the Goodhart drift and bikeshedding that plagued the pipeline architecture are structurally prevented. The auto-remediation loop is, in effect, the application of every principle described so far: contract-driven development, mechanical verification, sequential decomposition, stigmergic coordination through shared test results, and constraint topology that enforces correctness at the boundaries while leaving implementation freedom in the interior.

• • •

The comfortable response to this trajectory is to identify a task that AI cannot do and declare it the permanent domain of human engineers. The industry has proposed direction, strategy, creativity, and judgment as permanent human contributions, each offered with the confidence of someone drawing a line on a map and calling it a border. Understanding what to build, understanding whether what was built is correct: these too have been proposed, at various points in the last three years, as the irreducible human contribution that AI will never replicate.

Each of these proposals has a problem, which is that the boundary it draws is not stable. AI systems that interact with customer support channels can identify the features users request most frequently. AI systems with access to market data can perform the analysis that informs strategic decisions. AI systems that monitor production behavior through stigmergic signals can identify the problems that need solving without a human's needing to name them. The auto-remediation loop described above includes specification generation, which is the formalization of what the system should do, the activity that was supposed to be the engineer's primary contribution. Each time the industry draws a line and says "but humans will always do this," the line moves, because the line is defined by current capability rather than by any structural limit, and current capability changes faster than the industry's ability to recalibrate its assumptions.

The honest accounting also requires acknowledging where the current limitations are structural rather than developmental. Peer-reviewed research has demonstrated that transformer architectures struggle with function composition, the very operation that lies at the heart of software engineering, with performance declining rapidly as the depth of composition increases. A January 2026 paper titled "Why Reasoning Fails to Plan" showed that chain-of-thought reasoning is greedy local optimization: it selects locally plausible actions but cannot reshape early decisions based on downstream consequences, which means that once an architectural commitment is made, the model cannot revise it when later evidence shows it was wrong. Models exhibit a 64.5 percent blind spot rate for their own errors, meaning they can fix errors identified by external sources but cannot detect or correct their own mistakes, and this self-verification capability does not improve with stronger generation ability. Apple's "Illusion of Thinking" study found that reasoning models show an effort paradox: reasoning effort increases with problem complexity up to a point, then declines even when the model has adequate token budget, suggesting that the models are performing increasingly strained pattern matching rather than executing algorithms. These are not temporary limitations waiting for the next model release to resolve. They are properties of the current architecture, and while future architectures may address them, the history of AI development is that solving one class of limitation typically reveals the next.

This is not an argument that AI will do everything. It is an argument that every specific task you name as the human contribution is a poor foundation for a career strategy, because the set of tasks AI can perform is expanding and the expansion follows a pattern that is predictable even if the specific tasks are not. The pattern is: tasks with clear specifications and mechanical verification migrate first. Tasks with fuzzy specifications and judgment-dependent verification migrate second, as models develop the ability to handle ambiguity and as organizations develop the infrastructure to provide the contextual information that fuzzy tasks require. Tasks that require access to dispersed, tacit, contextual knowledge migrate last, because the information infrastructure required to surface that knowledge and make it accessible to an AI system is the most expensive and most organizationally difficult to build.

The distinction between "last to migrate" and "will never migrate" is worth dwelling on, because conflating the two is the most common source of false comfort in the current discourse. "Last" means that the information infrastructure required to automate a task is expensive, organizationally difficult, and slow to build, not that the task contains some irreducible quality that resists automation in principle. The tasks that require dispersed, tacit knowledge will migrate last because surfacing that knowledge, encoding it, and making it accessible to an automated system is a harder engineering problem than generating code from a specification. Harder is not impossible. The engineer who builds a career strategy on the assumption that judgment, context-sensitivity, or organizational navigation will remain permanently human is making the same category of error as the engineer who assumed, five years ago, that code generation would remain permanently human. The correct career strategy is not to identify a task and declare it safe. It is to develop the ability to reason about the forces that govern all tasks, so that when the specific task you occupy is automated, the understanding that produced your competence transfers to whatever comes next.

• • •

The invariants are the physics that does not change regardless of which tasks migrate and when. There are five of them, and they are worth restating in the context of trajectory because they are the foundation of whatever comes next.

Coordination has costs. The $O(n^2)$ scaling of dialogue-based coordination, the information loss at every handoff boundary, the Crawford-Sobel degradation in every communication channel where sender and receiver have different incentive functions. These costs are properties of information transmission between agents, and they apply regardless of whether the agents are human, artificial, or a combination. A system of a thousand AI agents coordinating through dialogue will experience the same scaling costs as a system of a thousand humans, because the costs are not properties of the substrate. They are properties of the coordination mechanism. The DeepMind and MIT study on scaling agent systems, published in December 2025, confirmed this with empirical precision: multi-agent systems exhibit a two-to-six-times efficiency penalty with more than ten tools, error amplification of 17.2 times in independent agent configurations (reduced to 4.4 times with centralized coordination), and sequential reasoning degradation of thirty-nine to seventy percent across every multi-agent variant tested. UC Berkeley's failure taxonomy, presented at ICLR 2025, identified fourteen unique failure modes across five popular multi-agent frameworks, with failure rates reaching 86.7 percent. The coordination physics is not a theoretical concern. It is an empirical finding that scales with the substrate.

Proxies drift from objectives. Goodhart's Law operates on any measurable intermediate representation, whether the measurement is performed by a human, an AI model, or an automated dashboard. Test suites are proxies for correctness. Contracts are proxies for requirements. Monitoring metrics are proxies for system health. The gap between proxy and objective exists because the objective is a property of the real world and the proxy is a property of the measurement system, and no measurement system has infinite resolution. The gap can be minimized through iterative, evidence-driven refinement. It cannot be eliminated.

Information degrades through layers. The Data Processing Inequality guarantees that every processing step in a communication chain loses information, and the lost information cannot be recovered by subsequent processing. This applies to hierarchical organizations, to multi-agent AI architectures, to any system that compresses high-dimensional reality into lower-dimensional representations for transmission or storage. The engineer who understands this can design systems that minimize the number of layers and maximize the fidelity of each layer. The engineer who does not understand this will continue to add layers (more review stages, more governance processes, more coordination mechanisms) and be puzzled when the additional layers make things worse.

The specification gap never closes. The distance between what someone wants and what they can articulate is permanent, because wanting is a property of a complex system (a person, an organization, a market) and articulation is a compression of that complexity into language. The compression is lossy, for the same information-theoretic reasons that all compression is lossy. No amount of requirements gathering, no number of stakeholder interviews, no sophistication of specification tools will produce a specification that captures the full complexity of what the system is supposed to do, because the full complexity includes edge cases that no one has imagined, interactions that no one has anticipated, and behaviors that no one will recognize as requirements until the system fails to exhibit them. The specification gap is the reason that epistemological gates exist, the reason that production monitoring is necessary even when all tests pass, and the reason that the auto-remediation loop includes a diagnosis step that discovers requirements the original specification did not contain. There is a related asymmetry that Jason Wei at OpenAI has articulated precisely: code correctness can be checked via tests, types, and formal methods, which makes code the best domain for reinforcement learning training, which explains why coding benchmarks improve fastest. But the things that matter most in production, architectural soundness, maintainability, operational resilience, security posture, are the hardest to auto-verify. No test suite exists for good architecture. The capabilities that improve fastest under current training methods are the capabilities that matter least for system-level engineering, and the capabilities that matter most are the ones that resist the training signal that drives improvement. This is not a bug in the training process. It is a consequence of the verification asymmetry, and it will persist as long as the things we care most about are the things we cannot mechanically specify.

Cognitive and computational limits are real. Context windows, attention dilution, the effective capacity of working memory whether biological or silicon: these are physical constraints on information processing that determine how much complexity any single agent can manage simultaneously. The limits shift as technology improves (context windows grow, attention mechanisms become more efficient, processing capacity increases), but the existence of limits does not change, and the engineering response to limits, decomposition, compression, abstraction, constraint design, remains necessary regardless of where the specific limits fall.

• • •

What does it mean to understand these invariants? It means that the engineer who has absorbed the physics can reason about any configuration of the landscape, including configurations that do not yet exist, because the reasoning is grounded in forces that are permanent rather than in capabilities that are transient. When a new AI system claims to solve the coordination problem, the engineer who understands Crawford-Sobel can evaluate whether the system actually reduces signal degradation or merely moves it to a different channel. When a new metric is proposed as a measure of AI system quality, the engineer who understands Goodhart can predict whether the metric will survive optimization pressure or collapse under it. When a new architecture distributes work across agents, the engineer who understands the Data Processing Inequality can assess whether the distribution will preserve the information necessary for the parts to compose correctly or whether it will lose that information at the boundaries.

This ability to reason from principles rather than from recipes is the competency that does not expire when the recipes change. The specific practices, the context engineering techniques, the constraint design patterns, the coordination architectures, will evolve as the tools evolve. The principles that govern those practices, the information theory, the coordination costs, the cognitive limits, the Goodhart dynamics, will not evolve, because they are not properties of the current technology. They are properties of the physics of information, coordination, and constraint, and physics does not have release cycles.

• • •

The data above paints a picture that is simultaneously more nuanced and more unsettling than either the optimists or the pessimists acknowledge: the tools are not yet delivering the productivity gains the industry expects, but the rate of improvement in the tools is faster than the rate at which engineers can retool their skills, and the gap between those two rates is the landscape's defining feature.

The current state of AI-assisted engineering is one of productive confusion. The METR study, the most rigorous productivity measurement to date, found that experienced developers using AI tools were nineteen percent slower than those working without them, while the developers themselves believed they were twenty percent faster, a thirty-nine percent perception gap. The DORA 2025 report found that AI adoption had a positive relationship with delivery throughput but a negative relationship with delivery stability, with gains in delivery speed "largely cancelled out by a rise in the change failure rate." Veracode's 2025 analysis found that forty-five percent of AI-generated code contained OWASP Top 10 security vulnerabilities, with the rate reaching seventy-two percent for Java. A separate study by Shukla, Joshi, and Syed found that iteratively asking AI to fix its own security issues made the security posture worse, with critical vulnerabilities increasing by 37.6 percent after five iterations. These findings do not mean AI tools are useless. They mean that the tools amplify whatever engineering discipline is or is not present in the organization that adopts them, which is precisely the DORA report's conclusion: AI magnifies the strengths of high-performing organizations and the dysfunctions of struggling ones.

The ratio of humans to software is going to change. It is already changing. When the cost of producing a feature drops by an order of magnitude, the economic logic that justified a team of twelve engineers for a single product no longer holds. The logic that replaces it is not "twelve engineers, each ten times more productive." It is closer to "two engineers who understand the system's physics and the organizational context, supported by AI systems that handle the implementation, testing, maintenance, and much of the specification." The world will not need fewer engineers in the absolute sense, because the Jevons paradox applies: when the cost of producing software drops, the demand for software increases, because applications that were previously too expensive to build become economically viable. The total quantity of software produced will increase. The ratio of humans to units of software produced will decrease, dramatically, and the decrease will not be distributed evenly. The engineers who understand the physics will be the ones who remain, because they are the ones who can design the systems that the AI implements. The engineers who were valuable primarily for their ability to produce code, the accidental complexity that Brooks identified fifty years ago as the part that tools would eliminate, are competing with tools that produce code faster, cheaper, and at a quality that improves with every quarter.

This is not a prediction that engineers are obsolete. It is an observation that the definition of "engineer" is contracting around the essential complexity that was always the real work, and expanding away from the accidental complexity that occupied the majority of the profession's time. The contraction is painful for the people whose skills are concentrated in the accidental complexity. The expansion is an opportunity for the people whose skills are concentrated in the essential complexity, or who are willing to develop those skills.

The odds, honestly stated, are not in your favor. The transition is faster than most career-development timelines. The skills it requires are deep and take time to develop, and the development requires the kind of deliberate, sometimes uncomfortable engagement with complexity that is the precondition for genuine understanding. You cannot accelerate the grokking. You cannot shortcut the struggle. You can understand what to struggle with and why the struggle is productive.

• • •

The world has changed shape before, and the people inside the change never had the luxury of knowing what the new shape would be. The guild system gave way to factories. The typing pool gave way to word processors. The switchboard operator became a memory. In each transition, the familiar form of the work dissolved, and the dissolution was real loss for real people who had built competence and identity around that form. In each transition, the people who understood the forces at work found new ways to be valuable that nobody had imagined before the transition began, because the forces themselves created the demand for new kinds of contribution, and understanding the forces was the prerequisite for seeing the demand before it was obvious.

The familiar shape of the engineering job is dissolving. The engineer who spent a career mastering the accidental complexity, the syntax, the framework migrations, the build system configurations, the thousand small mechanical tasks that accumulated into a profession, is watching that accumulation lose its economic weight. That loss deserves to be named honestly: these were not bad engineers. Nobody wakes up with the goal of doing a bad job. They built competence in the work the profession asked them to do, and the profession changed what it was asking. The melancholy is appropriate. The essential complexity that was always the real work, the specification, the verification, the coordination, the judgment about whether the system does what it should do in a world that cannot fully articulate what it wants, is not shrinking. It is expanding, because every problem that was too expensive to solve with hand-written code becomes solvable when code is cheap, and every solvable problem needs someone who understands the physics well enough to ensure it is solved correctly. The demand for that understanding is growing faster than the tools that created the demand.

This book has given you the physics. It has not given you a guarantee, because the honest assessment of a landscape changing this fast does not support guarantees. What it has given you is a map of the forces that govern the territory, and the territory will be navigated by the people who understand those forces, because it always has been. The profession has always attracted people who are energized rather than paralyzed when the problem is hard and the stakes are real. The problem is hard. The stakes are real. The physics does not expire.

Acknowledgments

The experiments described in Part I were conducted over several months of iterative design, failure analysis, and redesign. The coordination architectures that failed so instructively did so because the experimental framework was rigorous enough to make the failures visible and measurable, and that rigor was the product of extensive prior work on the substrate-independent dysfunction hypothesis.

The coaching transcripts that inform Part V represent hundreds of hours of conversation with working engineers who allowed their struggles, their reasoning, and their growth to be documented and examined. The engineers whose sessions appear in these pages, anonymized but faithfully represented, demonstrated the kind of honest engagement with difficulty that the book argues is the foundation of genuine understanding. Their willingness to think out loud, to be wrong, and to revise their thinking in real time produced the empirical evidence for the human side of the argument.

The theoretical framework draws on decades of work by researchers whose contributions the references acknowledge individually. Crawford and Sobel's analysis of strategic information transmission, Goodhart's observation about the corruption of measurement, Shannon's formalization of information, Kapur's empirical work on productive failure, and Grassé's identification of stigmergic coordination each provided a load-bearing element of the argument. The synthesis is mine; the foundations are theirs.

The ideas in this book were developed in conversation with systems, with organizations, and with the daily practice of building software under real constraints. The Pact and Emergence systems served as laboratories where the theoretical principles could be tested against the resistance of working code and real coordination problems. The dysfunction experiments served as the controlled environment where the failures could be isolated, measured, and attributed to specific structural causes.

This book was written during a period of genuine uncertainty about the profession's future, and that uncertainty is itself a condition shared with the reader. The argument did not arrive from a position of detached certainty. It was written by someone navigating the same landscape the reader is navigating, with the same imperfect information, trying to identify the forces that are permanent in a field where almost everything else is transient. If the book's honesty about what it does not know is occasionally uncomfortable, that discomfort is the same discomfort the author experienced in writing it, and the same discomfort that anyone thinking clearly about this transition should expect to feel.

References

Foundational Theory

Brooks, F.P. (1975). *The Mythical Man-Month: Essays on Software Engineering*. Addison-Wesley. The distinction between accidental and essential complexity that Chapter 1 argues is newly visible when code production costs collapse.

Collins, A.M., & Loftus, E.F. (1975). A Spreading-Activation Theory of Semantic Processing. *Psychological Review*, 82(6), 407-428. The associative memory model that Chapter 12 uses to explain the mechanism of grokking.

Crawford, V.P., & Sobel, J. (1982). Strategic Information Transmission. *Econometrica*, 50(6), 1431-1451. The formal model of signal degradation in communication between agents with different incentive functions, applied in Chapters 2, 10, and 14.

Goodhart, C.A.E. (1975). Problems of Monetary Management: The U.K. Experience. *Papers in Monetary Economics*, Reserve Bank of Australia. The observation that proxy metrics collapse under optimization pressure, central to Chapter 11.

Grassé, P.-P. (1959). La reconstruction du nid et les coordinations interindividuelles chez *Bellicositermes natalensis* et *Cubitermes sp*. *Insectes Sociaux*, 6(1), 41-80. The identification and naming of stigmergic coordination, the foundation of Chapter 9.

Kapur, M. (2016). Examining Productive Failure, Productive Success,

Unproductive Failure, and Unproductive Success in Learning. *Educational Psychologist*, 51(2), 289-299. The empirical evidence (effect size d=0.36) that struggle before instruction produces deeper understanding, central to Chapter 12.

Liberti, J.M., & Mian, A.R. (2009). Estimating the Effect of Hierarchies on Information Use. *Review of Financial Studies*, 22(10), 4057-4090. The empirical finding that soft information dies at the third level of organizational hierarchy, applied in Chapter 10.

Miller, G.A. (1956). The Magical Number Seven, Plus or Minus Two: Some Limits on Our Capacity for Processing Information. *Psychological Review*, 63(2), 81-97. The cognitive capacity constraints that Chapter 7 applies to decomposition design and Chapter 10 applies to hierarchical coordination.

Shannon, C.E. (1948). A Mathematical Theory of Communication. *Bell System Technical Journal*, 27(3), 379-423. The formalization of information theory that underlies the Data Processing Inequality, applied throughout Parts II, III, and IV.

Strathern, M. (1997). 'Improving Ratings': Audit in the British University System. *European Review*, 5(3), 305-321. The reformulation of Goodhart's Law that Chapter 11 uses as its operating definition.

Tishby, N., Pereira, F.C., & Bialek, W. (2000). The Information Bottleneck Method. *Proceedings of the 37th Annual Allerton Conference on Communication, Control, and Computing*. The compression framework that Chapter 5 applies to context management.

Industry Research and Reports

Shojaee, P., Mirzadeh, I., Alizadeh, K., Horton, M., Bengio, S., & Farajtabar, M. (2025). The Illusion of Thinking: Understanding the Strengths and Limitations of Reasoning Models via the Lens of Problem Complexity. Apple Research. arXiv:2506.06941. Analysis of reasoning model behavior showing the effort paradox: reasoning effort increases with complexity up to a threshold, then declines despite adequate token budget. Referenced in Chapter 17.

Harvey, N., DeBellis, D., Storer, K., Beane, M., Edwards, R., et al. (2025). *DORA State of AI-Assisted Software Development Report*. Google Cloud. https://cloud.google.com/resources/content/2025-dora-ai-assisted-software-development-report. Finding that AI adoption correlates positively with delivery throughput but negatively with delivery stability, with gains in delivery speed "largely cancelled out by a rise in the change failure rate." Referenced in Chapters 1 and 17.

Becker, J., Rush, N., Barnes, E., & Rein, D. (2025). Measuring the Impact of Early-2025 AI on Experienced Open-Source Developer Productivity. METR.

arXiv:2507.09089. Randomized controlled trial with 16 experienced developers across 246 tasks, finding 19% slower completion with AI tools despite developer prediction of 24% speedup. Referenced in Chapters 1, 5, and 17.

Mao, K., Kapus, T., Åhs, C.T., Marescotti, M., Ip, D., Hajdu, Á., Cela, S., & Banerjee, A. (2025). WhatsCode: Large-Scale GenAI Deployment for Developer Efficiency at WhatsApp. ICSE-SEIP '26. arXiv:2512.05314. Documentation of a 25-month deployment processing 3,000+ accepted code changes, with a stable 60/40 ratio of single-click acceptance to human-guided modification. Referenced in Chapter 17.

Cemri, M., Pan, M.Z., Yang, S., Agrawal, L.A., Chopra, B., Tiwari, R., Keutzer, K., Parameswaran, A., Klein, D., Ramchandran, K., Zaharia, M., Gonzalez, J.E., & Stoica, I. (2025). Why Do Multi-Agent LLM Systems Fail? ICLR 2025 Building Trust Workshop. arXiv:2503.13657. Identification of 14 unique failure modes across five multi-agent frameworks, with failure rates reaching 86.7%. Referenced in Chapter 17.

Veracode (2025). 2025 GenAI Code Security Report: Assessing the Security of Using LLMs for Coding. https://www.veracode.com/resources/analyst-reports/2025-genai-code-security-report/. Finding that 45% of AI-generated code contained OWASP Top 10 vulnerabilities (72% for Java). Referenced in Chapter 17.

Shukla, S., Joshi, H., & Syed, R. (2025). Security Degradation in Iterative AI Code Generation — A Systematic Analysis of the Paradox. arXiv:2506.11022. Finding that iteratively asking AI to fix its own security issues increases critical vulnerabilities by 37.6% after five iterations. Referenced in Chapter 17.

AI Capability and Scaling Research

Xiao, C., Cai, J., Zhao, W., Zeng, G., Lin, B., Zhou, J., Zheng, Z., Han, X., Liu, Z., & Sun, M. (2025). Densing Law of LLMs. *Nature Machine Intelligence*, 7, 1823-1833. Documentation of "capability density" (capability per parameter) as a metric, finding it doubles approximately every three months. Referenced in Chapter 17.

Kim, Y., Gu, K., Park, C., Park, C., Schmidgall, S., Heydari, A.A., Yan, Y., Zhang, Z., Zhuang, Y., Malhotra, M., Liang, P.P., Park, H.W., Yang, Y., Xu, X., Du, Y., Patel, S., Althoff, T., McDuff, D., & Liu, X. (2025). Towards a Science of Scaling Agent Systems. Google DeepMind & MIT. arXiv:2512.08296. Empirical study finding 2-6x efficiency penalty with more than ten tools, 17.2x error amplification in independent agent configurations (4.4x with centralized coordination), and 39-70% sequential reasoning degradation across multi-agent variants. Referenced in Chapters 7 and 17.

Wang, Z., Wu, F., Wang, H., Tang, X., Li, B., Yin, Z., Ma, Y., Li, Y., Sun,

W., Chen, X., & Ye, Y. (2026). Why Reasoning Fails to Plan: A Planning-Centric Analysis of Long-Horizon Decision Making in LLM Agents. *arXiv preprint*, arXiv:2601.22311. Analysis demonstrating that chain-of-thought reasoning performs greedy local optimization, selecting locally plausible actions without the ability to revise early decisions based on downstream consequences. Referenced in Chapter 17.

Cognitive Science

Leroy, S. (2009). Why Is It So Hard to Do My Work? The Challenge of Attention Residue when Switching Between Work Tasks. *Organizational Behavior and Human Decision Processes*, 109(2), 168-181. The finding that attention patterns activated during a cognitive task persist after transition to a subsequent task, degrading performance on the second task. Applied in Chapters 5 and 13.

Dunbar, R.I.M. (1992). Neocortex Size as a Constraint on Group Size in Primates. *Journal of Human Evolution*, 22(6), 469-493. The cognitive limit on the number of stable social relationships, applied in Chapter 10.

Sharma, M., Tong, M., Korbak, T., Duvenaud, D., Askell, A., Bowman, S.R., et al. (2024). Towards Understanding Sycophancy in Language Models. In *Proceedings of the Twelfth International Conference on Learning Representations (ICLR 2024)*. Research finding significant accuracy drops when user suggestions contain incorrect answers, demonstrating that models trade accuracy for agreement. Referenced in Chapter 5.

WHO Surgical Safety Checklist. Haynes, A.B., et al. (2009). A Surgical Safety Checklist to Reduce Morbidity and Mortality in a Global Population. *New England Journal of Medicine*, 360(5), 491-499. The finding that structured decomposition of surgical concerns reduced mortality by 47%, applied in Chapter 13.

Historical Cases

Deepwater Horizon explosion and oil spill (2010). *Report to the President: National Commission on the BP Deepwater Horizon Oil Spill and Offshore Drilling*. Eleven workers killed and 4 million barrels of oil released after engineers failed to translate anomalous negative pressure test results into the decision frame of the well site leaders who controlled the proceed-or-halt decision. Referenced in Chapters 14 and 15.

Hyatt Regency walkway collapse (1981, Kansas City). *National Bureau of Standards Investigation of the Kansas City Hyatt Regency Walkway Collapse (NBS Building Science Series 143)*. One hundred fourteen deaths resulting from a fabrication change to hanger rod design that doubled the load on an upper walkway connection, approved through a shop-drawing review process without recalculation. Referenced in Chapter 1.

Healthcare.gov launch failure (2013). Federal investigation documenting the consequences of parallel development without coordination discipline. Referenced in Chapter 1.

Knight Capital Group trading incident (2012). SEC filing documenting $460 million in losses within 45 minutes from an automated trading system deployed without adequate verification. Referenced in Chapter 1.

Atlanta Public Schools cheating scandal (2009–2015). Georgia Governor's Special Investigators report and subsequent RICO trial documenting how 178 educators across 44 schools systematically altered standardized test answers in response to accountability metrics tied to No Child Left Behind. Referenced in Chapter 11.

Presidential Task Force on Market Mechanisms (1988). *Report of the Presidential Task Force on Market Mechanisms* (The Brady Report). U.S. Government Printing Office. Investigation of the 1987 stock market crash documenting how automated program trading accelerated the collapse, leading to the implementation of circuit breakers as mechanical constraints on trading activity. Referenced in Chapter 8.

Works by the Author

McEntire, J. (2026). *The Cage and the Mirror: How to Make Rigid Organizations Resilient Again*. Cage & Mirror Publishing. ISBN 979-8-9940343-4-7. Examination of organizational dysfunction through variance compression, Godelian incompleteness, and the iron cage, referenced in Chapter 15.

McEntire, J. (2026). Substrate-Independent Dysfunction: Coordination Failure as Information-Theoretic Constraint. Manuscript under review. The controlled experiments in multi-agent AI coordination that provide the empirical foundation for Chapters 2, 6, 7, 9, 10, and 11.

Additional References

Feynman, R.P. (1974). Cargo Cult Science. Caltech commencement address. Reprinted in *Surely You're Joking, Mr. Feynman!* (1985), W.W. Norton. The distinction between imitating the form of the scientific method and practicing its substance. Referenced in Chapters 11, 12, 15, and 17.

Heinlein, R.A. (1961). *Stranger in a Strange Land*. Putnam. Origin of the term "grok," used in Chapter 12 to name the phenomenon of deep, generative understanding.

Wei, J. (2025). Asymmetry of Verification and Verifier's Rule. https://www.jasonwei.net/blog/asymmetry-of-verification-and-verifiers-law. Observation that code correctness is mechanically verifiable, making it the best domain for reinforcement learning, while the qualities that matter most for system-level engineering (architectural soundness, maintainability, security posture) resist auto-verification. Referenced in Chapter 17.

About the Author

Jeremy McEntire has spent his career at the intersection of software engineering, organizational dynamics, and the coordination problems that determine whether complex systems produce value or consume it. His work bridges theory and practice in a way that is unusual in either domain: he builds the systems, runs the experiments, and writes the analysis.

His multi-agent AI research produced four distinct coordination architectures — Pact (contract-first mechanical verification), Swarm (formation-driven autonomous engineering), Emergence (stigmergic decentralized coordination), and Apprentice (adaptive model distillation) — each designed to test a specific hypothesis about when and why multi-agent systems fail. The controlled comparison of these architectures, using the same language model, the same task, and the same budget, produced the empirical findings that anchor this book: the eighty-seven percent rejection rate, the verification theater, the specification perfectionism, and the monotonic inverse correlation between coordination complexity and output quality. The results are formalized in his paper on substrate-independent dysfunction, which demonstrates that the coordination failures observed in AI systems are governed by the same information-theoretic constraints (Crawford-Sobel signal degradation, Goodhart proxy drift, the Data Processing Inequality) that produce identical patterns in human organizations.

Pact, the contract-first framework, has over nine hundred tests and includes production auto-remediation: when monitored code fails, the system spawns a fixer agent with full contract context, adds a reproducer test to the specification, and rebuilds the module. The contract gets stricter; the next implementation cannot have that bug. Apprentice manages the lifecycle of distilling knowledge from expensive frontier models into specialized local models, with adaptive coaching that detects quality drift through rolling-window correlation and adjusts sampling frequency as a continuous function of measured confidence. These are not prototypes. They are working systems designed to operate at the boundary where AI capability meets coordination reality.

Before the research, McEntire spent two decades building systems at scale. At Twilio, he created the Edge Services organization from inception to sixteen engineers across three teams, maintaining 99.999% API uptime for fifteen billion weekly requests across nine global data centers. He holds three US patents for edge infrastructure (handshake optimization, adaptive throttling, edge delivery management) and a pending patent for stigmergic mesh architecture. At Wander, he inherited a platform with daily database outages, stabilized it, and designed a seven-service backend assessed as top five percent of the short-term rental industry for infrastructure quality. He has led teams from five to forty across cybersecurity, marketplace, AdTech, and luxury authentication platforms.

He is the author of five books, including *The Cage and the Mirror* (organizational dysfunction through the lens of Godelian incompleteness) and *Privacy: Architecture of Forgetting* (cryptographic architecture for privacy-preserving internet infrastructure). His academic papers, available on arXiv and SSRN, include work on stigmergic mesh architectures, organizational incompleteness theory, and dysmemic pressure. He studied pure mathematics at the University of Oklahoma, which is where the comfort with information theory comes from.

The coaching transcripts that inform the chapters on grokking, multi-pass thinking, and translating between technical and business frames come from years of working with engineers through the organizational forces that the book's theoretical framework describes. The multi-agent systems that provide the empirical evidence are tools he built and uses. The failures he analyzes are failures he produced, measured, and then designed around. The book is written from the inside of the problem.